As one of the world's longest established
and best-known travel brands,
Thomas Cook are the experts in travel.

For more than 135 years our
guidebooks have unlocked the secrets
of destinations around the world,
sharing with travellers a wealth of
experience and a passion for travel.

**Rely on Thomas Cook as your
travelling companion on your next trip
and benefit from our unique heritage.**

Thomas Cook **pocket** guides

GOTHENBURG

Written by Marc Di Duca, updated by Caroline Hainer

Published by Thomas Cook Publishing
A division of Thomas Cook Tour Operations Limited
Company registration no. 3772199 England
The Thomas Cook Business Park, Unit 9, Coningsby Road,
Peterborough PE3 8SB, United Kingdom
Email: books@thomascook.com, Tel: +44 (0) 1733 416477
www.thomascookpublishing.com

Produced by Cambridge Publishing Management Limited
Burr Elm Court, Main Street, Caldecote CB23 7NU
www.cambridgepm.co.uk

ISBN: 978-1-84848-407-8

© 2007, 2009 Thomas Cook Publishing
This third edition © 2011 Thomas Cook Publishing
Text © Thomas Cook Publishing
Maps © Thomas Cook Publishing/PCGraphics (UK) Limited
Transport map © Communicarta Limited

Series Editor: Karen Beaulah
Production/DTP: Steven Collins

Printed and bound in Spain by GraphyCems

Cover photography © age fotostock/SuperStock

CONTENTS

SYMBOLS KEY

The following symbols are used throughout this book:

ⓐ address ☎ telephone ⓦ website address ⓔ email
🕐 opening times Ⓝ public transport connections ❶ important

The following symbols are used on the maps:

𝒊	information office	O	city
🛪	airport	O	large town
🛡	police station	○	small town
🚍	bus station	=	motorway
🚆	railway station	—	main road
✝	cathedral		minor road
	point of interest	—	railway
❶	numbers denote featured cafés & restaurants		

Hotels and restaurants are graded by approximate price as follows:
£ budget price **££** mid-range price **£££** expensive

⊙ *The fine old buildings of Gustav Adolfs Torg by the Stora Hamn Canal*

INTRODUCING
Gothenburg

Introduction

It's hard not to like Gothenburg (Göteborg in Swedish, pronounced *yurtebor*) on Sweden's west coast. Strolling its bustling cobbled streets and grand 19th-century boulevards, visitors encounter the sights, sounds and smells that make the city unique: the blue trams rumbling through the city, their wheels grinding the shallow rails and their motors whining as they climb the city's hills; the inviting, comforting, familiar fragrance of coffee, cinnamon and freshly baked cakes and bread wafting from every café doorway; and funkily dressed Gothenburgers pressing their noses against shop windows, their rosy faces illuminated by the sparkling goods on show. Scandinavian order prevails, the streets are safe and the English-speaking population helpful and genuinely friendly. The energy of trade and commerce still has a hold on everyday life, making the city a wonderful source of retail therapy.

Gothenburg is also a city of superlatives – it boasts the biggest film festival in the Nordic region, the largest tram network, Sweden's largest university, Scandinavia's biggest shopping centre, the Nordic countries' largest amusement park at Liseberg, the world's biggest maritime museum, the biggest hotel in the Nordic region and the busiest port. This is a city that certainly doesn't do things by halves.

You'll find Sweden's second city is just a little bit friendlier and more accessible than the capital. The public transport system is one of the finest you'll encounter in Europe, and accommodation, though expensive, is of a high standard. Where Gothenburg really comes into its own, however, is in its lively café culture and first-rate seafood restaurants. Add to these a sprinkling of attention-grabbing museums, including the fine City Art Museum, countless parks and several exciting nightspots, and Gothenburg – not a wholly discovered destination – shapes up as an ideal place to sample the best this wonderful country has to offer.

● *Take a boat trip past the Feskekôrka indoor market*

When to go

SEASONS & CLIMATE

In summer the weather is mild and the days are long. Around midsummer it is light for about 18 hours a day. The light and warmth entice people out on to the streets and into the cafés of Haga, and it seems the party never stops. This is also the season to catch some rays on the beaches of the Bohuslän Coast or south of Gothenburg in the resort of Varberg.

In winter/early spring and late autumn/early winter the weather can be dreary with leaden skies and incessant drizzle. Days are short, and the sun becomes something of a rarity. Of course, at this time of year cosy cafés and pubs draw you in and festive activity transforms the city.

● *Kämpebron – one of the oldest bridges in Gothenburg*

Gothenburg is a city of parks where the trees turn a fiery mix of reds and golds. October is a beautiful time to visit any of its green expanses.

ANNUAL EVENTS
January
Gothenburg International Film Festival Gothenburg plays host to the biggest public film festival in Scandinavia, with around 450 films from 70 countries screened to well over 120,000 visitors. Nordic films play a prominent role. ⓦ www.giff.se

February
European Championship in Oyster Opening Chefs vie to be crowned European champion in this annual competition to find the speediest oyster opener. ⓐ Eriksbergshallen, Maskingatan ⓣ 031 779 11 11 ⓦ www.oysteropeningcompetition.com

May
GöteborgsVarvet (Gothenburg Half Marathon) An incredible 36,000 people grunt and puff their way every May around Gothenburg's half-marathon course. ⓦ www.goteborgs varvet.com (online entries and information)

June
Midsummer party & crayfish feast *Midsommar* is no longer celebrated exactly on the summer solstice but on the third Friday in June. What started as a pagan festival to celebrate the longest day of the year has become just another excuse to stay up all night, get drunk and eat crayfish, the festival's traditional dish.

CHRISTMAS MAGIC

After the dullness of late autumn, Gothenburg explodes into a festival of light in early December as people prepare for one of the most important holidays in Scandinavia – Christmas. There are candles in front of every door, and in mid-December the spectacular illuminations along the Avenyn are switched on. The Liseberg Amusement Park is illuminated by five million fairy lights. This is one of the best times to be in the city with the hustle and bustle of Christmas shoppers filling the streets and twinkling yuletide lights wherever you look. ❶ Bring plenty of winter woollies as the icy wind coming off the sea will chill you to the bone.

August

Gothenburg Culture Festival/Kulturkalaset Annual city festival with free concerts, culture, entertainment and activities. Ⓦ www.goteborgskalaset.se

Way Out West International music festival featuring acts such as The Chemical Brothers, The xx and Paul Weller. Ⓐ Slottsskogen city park Ⓦ www.wayoutwest.se

September

Start of the lobster season The lobster season on the Bohuslän Coast lasts from late September until 30 April. The celebrations to mark the beginning of the season take place on the first Monday after 20 September. Events take place up and down the coast with exquisite seafood at the centre of things.

December
Christmas in Gothenburg Late November through to New Year is one of the most vibrant times to find yourself in Sweden's second city (see box opposite). Swedes take the yuletide season seriously. *God Jul!*

PUBLIC HOLIDAYS
New Year's Day 1 Jan
Epiphany 6 Jan
Good Friday 22 Apr 2011; 6 Apr 2012
Easter Monday 25 Apr 2011; 9 Apr 2012
Walpurgis Night 30 Apr
May Day 1 May
Ascension Day May
Whit Sunday May/June
National Day 6 June
Midsummer's Eve 3rd Friday in June
All Saints' Day 1 Nov
Christmas Eve 24 Dec
Christmas Day 25 Dec
Boxing Day 26 Dec
New Year's Eve 31 Dec

Kulturkalaset (Gothenburg Culture Festival)

Possibly the most exciting time to travel to Gothenburg is early August when the city holds its annual city festival, a party to which everyone is invited. Two weeks of music, food, partying and copious amounts of alcohol in the warm summer air and almost round-the-clock daylight see this city's usually reserved and sensible population let their hair down and enjoy themselves. One of the best things about the whole caboodle is that all the organised events are free. Stages are set up on the city's major thoroughfares and squares, and top names from the world of Swedish rock and pop, as well as international acts, perform to throngs of revellers. There are all kinds of theatre and dance performances, and much drinking, eating and merrymaking follows. Food stalls selling scrumptious fare from Scandinavia and around the world line several streets, and ale is readily available in plastic beer glasses, one of the few times you will witness this in the city.

A slight downside to the proceedings is the amount of public drunkenness the festival generates. Alcohol and Swedes form a potentially volatile mix and there have been reports of the atmosphere late at night becoming threatening in the main streets. No wonder the state still maintains control over the sale of spirits and wine. Naturally, the vast majority of events at the festival pass off without trouble.

It goes without saying that accommodation will be completely booked up during the Kulturkalaset, so it's best to book early if you plan to arrive at this time. Ⓦ www.goteborgskalaset.se

● Nothing beats outdoor eating during Kulturkalaset

History

Vistors to Gothenburg might be a little surprised to discover that until the 17th century there was virtually nothing here, and it was only in 1621 that Gustav Adolf II ordered a city to be built. This was the fourth attempt to establish a Swedish 'gateway to the west', independent of Denmark, which controlled the west coast. The original city was designed by Dutch engineers and architects and occupied today's Inom Vallgraven. Only two canals remain from that time as most others have been filled in.

○ *The 17th-century New Älvsborg Fortress protected the emerging city*

Due to the ever-present threat of Danish attack, the emerging city was one of the most heavily fortified in the region. Much of the city was built of wood and, inevitably, devastating fires broke out on a disturbingly regular basis. On average, Gothenburg was reduced to ashes almost every 16 years between 1669 and 1804.

Gothenburg was a truly cosmopolitan city during the 18th and 19th centuries with many British, Dutch and German merchants making the city their home. Much of the trade flowing through the city came from the East, and for more than eight decades during the 19th century, commerce was dominated by the Swedish East India Company. Growing ever fatter on trade, Gothenburg burst out of its 17th-century canal belt and spread out in all directions.

William Chalmers was born in Gothenburg in 1748. He used his vast inheritance to found the Chalmers' Polytechnic and the Sahlgrenska hospital.

Alexander Keiller, a Scot, founded the Gothenburg shipyard in 1841, an industry that provided many jobs right up until the 1980s. Another Scot, Robert Dickson, was involved in trade in Gothenburg in the latter half of the 19th century, and he and his family subsequently became prominent philanthropists, building a library and almshouses in Haga.

Gothenburg is the principal centre of Sweden's export trade and the country's premier port. The Volvo factory still churns out thousands of vehicles a year, and tourism is a major contributor to municipal coffers. Gothenburg is also the home of many clothes companies and Swedish designers, including Nudie Jeans, Velour, Stylein and Permanent Vacation, which contribute to Gothenburg's trendy image.

Lifestyle

When observing everyday life in Sweden, words such as orderliness and self-restraint come immediately to mind. Cyclists stick religiously to cycle lanes, pedestrians to the pavement, the streets are litter-free, and it must be dull working the trams as an inspector since everyone has a ticket (except the odd confused tourist). People arrive on time for meetings, and Swedes take punctuality very seriously (and expect you to do likewise). You'd better have a good excuse if you arrive ten minutes after you promised. Shops open and close on time, every street has a well-marked name, every house a number, and everything ticks along just nicely. Despite the absence of chaos, nothing ever becomes over-the-top and flashy. As a result, dress manages to be both smart (with a concession to shabby-chic) and rather conservative.

Sadly, as is true in many countries, this all comes crashing down when alcohol is mixed into the equation. Drink is absurdly expensive, and this has a tendency to make some people binge when they get the opportunity. After a few units, a small minority of Swedes turn from mild-mannered, middle-class, consensus-loving model citizens into a somewhat more uninhibited proposition.

Swedes are a tolerant bunch and, up until recently, accepted refugees into the country in almost unlimited numbers. Gothenburg has a large immigrant population, mostly Kurds and Bosnians who arrived in the early- to mid-1990s. The average Swede may speak better English than you do, but don't expect refugees (who are probably struggling with Swedish) to do likewise.

Café culture plays a major role in day-to-day living in Gothenburg, especially among the 60,000 or more students (almost half of whom are from overseas) that the city hosts. From breakfast at SoHo to a buffet lunch at a small street café in Haga, to cocktails on the Avenyn at night, the city's cafés, pubs, bars and restaurants are busy around the clock, and people just love to sit, nibble, sip and chat with friends and colleagues. This is one of Gothenburg's most endearing qualities, and a side of local life that the visitor should partake of to the full.

● *Shoppers and tourists mingle in the spotlessly clean streets*

Culture

When it comes to culture, Gothenburg has much to offer and is second only to the capital, Stockholm, when it comes to opera and classical music – though don't say that in Gothenburg! Gothenburg's high-profile venues, the Konserthuset and the Gothenburg Opera House, provide the best of highbrow culture in the city. Compared to London or New York, ticket prices are relatively low and the standard of performances comparable. The Gothenburg Symphony Orchestra (GSO) was founded in 1905 and is now officially the National Orchestra of Sweden. It mostly performs works by Nordic composers at the Konserthuset but has also toured to great acclaim.

Musicals are big in Sweden at the moment, with productions of West End and Broadway favourites appearing on Swedish theatre stages. In many ways – and hardly surprisingly – the ball was set in motion by *Mamma Mia!*, which is based on ABBA songs and written by the male members of the band, Benny Andersson and Björn Ulvaeus, the latter a native of Gothenburg (see below).

GOTHENBURG'S MOST FAMOUS SON?

It's surprising that the city's tourist authorities don't make more of the fact that Björn Ulvaeus was born in Gothenburg on 25 April 1945. Ulvaeus was the mastermind behind much of ABBA's success (he was the one with the beard). He only spent the first 11 years of his life in Gothenburg before moving to Västervik, a small town on the east coast.

◆ *Gothenburg Opera House is an imposing sight*

Sweden's second city also enjoys a plethora of superb museums and galleries such as the City Museum, the Universeum Science Museum, the Art Museum and the Röhsska Design Museum. These are some of the best museums in the country and some of the highlights of any visit to the city.

In addition to regular programmes at the city's cultural venues, Gothenburg also hosts numerous annual events with a cultural flavour. The **Kulturkalaset** is the best opportunity to catch live bands on the streets, as well as other organised cultural acts and events. Most of them are free. Other significant cultural events are the Gothenburg Film Festival held in January, the Gothenburg Choir Festival in June, the Gothenburg Jazz Festival held in late August and the International Biennial for Contemporary Art, which takes place throughout the autumn.

Expect Swedes to be very knowledgeable about their own culture and that of the wider world. Most are well read and expect a high standard when it comes to the performing arts, which are still heavily subsidised by the state.

Gothenburg English Speaking Theatre Ⓦ www.gest.se
Gothenburg Opera Ⓦ http://en.opera.se
Gothenburg Symphony Orchestra & Concert Hall Ⓦ www.gso.se

Ⓞ *The Storan, near Kungsparken, is now used for concerts*

 MAKING THE MOST OF
Gothenburg

Shopping

It's no exaggeration to say that Gothenburg has some of the best shopping to be found north of London and south of the Arctic Circle. It is one of the city's main draws, attracting Swedes and foreign visitors alike, especially just prior to Christmas. Gothenburg offers a holistic shopping experience with the best outlets for hundreds of kilometres in every direction, pedestrianised shopping thoroughfares and a myriad of eateries to set down carrier bags and rest tired feet and debit cards over a light lunch or cup of coffee.

The **Nordstan** shopping centre (see page 67) likes to brag that it's the biggest in Scandinavia, and when you consider that it is the size of 55 football pitches, houses 150 shops and restaurants and even has its own Tourist Information Bureau, it may well have a point. It is divided into eight zones, and locating a map is an essential part of any visit. Across the street there is another gigantic complex of shops and cafés and in other parts of the city the Avenyn, pedestrianised

GOTHENBURG PASS

Purchasing the Gothenburg Pass entitles you to discounts at over 50 outlets, cafés and restaurants. These can range from SEK 100 off your purchase to a whopping 30 per cent discount. It can be purchased from tourist offices, hotels, hostels, Pressbyrån newsagents, Västtrafik's customer service booths, and many other places across the city.

◒ *If shopping malls are your bag, head to Nordstan*

Kungsgatan, Östra Hamngatan and Linnégatan are lined with every sort of shop you can imagine. The outlets along the Avenyn tend to be more exclusive, and the same is true of the Arkaden, Citypassagen and Kompassen centres opposite the Nordstan. If it's more offbeat, quainter shops you're after,

USEFUL SHOPPING PHRASES

How much is this?
Hur mycket kostar det här?
*Heur mewcket kostar
det hair?*

Do you have this in size ...?
Har ni den här i storlek ...?
*Haar nee den hair
ee stoorlehk ...?*

Can I try this on?
Kan jag prova den här?
Kun yaag proova den hair?

I'll take it
Jag tar den
Yaag taar den

wandering the cobbled lanes of Haga will produce results. The narrow streets are packed with craft boutiques, design emporia and second-hand bookshops galore.

Gothenburg has no single special item tourists buy as a reminder of their visit. The only real souvenirs that visitors take home are elk fridge magnets, elk key rings, Swedish flags or Dala Horses – colourful painted wooden figures, traditional for the Dalarna province. For kitsch-free traditional mementos, you could do a lot worse than head for Nordic Design Etc in the Nordstan Centre (zone 8). It specialises in traditional wood and cloth souvenirs, candlesticks and seasonal items with a folksy twist. The stock is expensive, but worth every öre.

Eating & drinking

Gothenburg is well known in European gourmet circles for its award-winning restaurants, particularly on the seafood front. Seafood fans will love the many Gothenburg eateries dedicated to *fruits de mer*, especially the Fiskekrogen and the small-scale diners at the Feskekôrka (Fish Church). No fewer than five of the city's restaurants have a star in the Michelin guide. Gothenburg chefs are regulars – and regularly do well – in prestigious culinary contests such as the Bocuse d'Or. Eating out here is no longer all about fish, meatballs and potatoes, and gastronomic influences from around the world can be seen and tasted at many of the local restaurants.

Menus are only occasionally in English, so some knowledge of the Swedish for basic, common dishes comes in handy. Menus begin with starters (*förrätter*), follow on with main dishes (*varmrätter*) and end with desserts (*desserter*). Characteristic Swedish dishes to look out for are *falukorv* (a kind of fat, pale hot dog), *köttbullar* (meatballs), *lövbiff* (strips of thinly sliced beef), gravadlax (marinated salmon), *ål* (eel), *sill* (herring), *pyttipanna* (diced fried meat, onions and boiled potatoes) and *kaviar* (red caviar). Away from the restaurant table, Swedes love their cheese

PRICE CATEGORIES

Average price for a main course at restaurants at the time of writing:

£ up to SEK 150   ££ SEK 150–225   £££ over SEK 225

◯ Enjoy fresh seafood from the counters at the Feskekôrka

and buy it by the kilogram slab at the supermarket. Jars of lingonberry and cloudberry jam, once vital sources of winter vitamin C, make tasty souvenirs.

Though prices have fallen a touch in the last decade, basically anything stronger than weak beer (3.5 per cent volume) in Sweden is pricey, to put it mildly. Indeed, wine and spirits can cost up to ten times what they do in the UK. Only beer can be bought from supermarkets; wines and spirits must be purchased on licensed premises or from special state-run shops, called *Systembolaget*, and only by those over 20 years of age. *Snaps* (*akvavit* or *aquavit*) and Absolut vodka are the quintessential Swedish firewaters. In winter don't miss a chance to down a few glasses of gut-warming *glögg* (mulled wine).

The Swedes are some of Europe's heaviest coffee-drinkers, meaning that devotees of the bean can look forward to top quality and a huge variety.

There's no denying that eating out anywhere in Sweden is a costly affair, but ways exist of filling your belly without emptying your wallet. Take full advantage of eat-till-you-burst hotel buffet breakfasts. At lunchtime almost every eatery (except fast-food joints) offers some kind of low-cost buffet lunch for local office workers, which can cost as little as SEK 60. Having got through enough food by 13.00 to last two days, you won't be hungry even when evening falls, and if you are, self-catering with supermarket picnic fare or a bite to eat in a pub, café or the Saluhallen food market (see page 64) will cost you just a few kronor.

It seems as though the golden 'M' of the McDonald's™ restaurant chain illuminates every street, and indeed, there are an incredible 25 branches throughout the city. Despite the

USEFUL DINING PHRASES

A table for two, please
Ett bord för två, tack
Et boord fur tvaw, tuck

The bill, please?
Kan jag få notan, tack?
Kun yaag faw nootan, tuck?

Waiter!/Waitress!
Ursäkta!
Eurshekta!

Where are the toilets?
Var är toaletten?
Vaar air tooaletten?

popularity and affordability of this brand of fast food, waistlines in Gothenburg remain on the slender side.

Booking ahead at popular restaurants is advisable, but not essential. Restaurants usually serve a lunch buffet from around 11.30 until 14.00, after which they may close until around 17.00, when they begin to serve dinner. You can usually order a meal until sometime between 22.00 and 23.00. Waiters may curse you from behind the bar if you don't leave a tip, but adding a tip of about ten per cent to the bill shows you were satisfied with the meal and service.

A pleasant aspect of eating out across Sweden is that all restaurants, pubs, clubs and bars are now smoke-free.

Entertainment & nightlife

Gothenburg is probably not the first place that pops into the mind when thinking about nightlife in Scandinavia; nevertheless, the city has a fairly vibrant club scene and countless other ways of spending an evening out on the tiles. Most of the clubs and discos can be found around the Avenyn, which, after dark, becomes the focus of the city's nightlife. A whole host of places provide bars to prop up for a couple of pre-club drinks, and if you find yourself with the munchies afterwards there's always Tintin, a 24-hour café just off the Avenyn. While the Gothenburg scene could hardly be described as wild, pleasure-seekers and clubbers will certainly not be left watching Swedish TV in their hotel rooms.

If you are heading out on the town, be sure to clear this with your bank manager first. The price of drinks in some clubs borders on the extortionate, and even just to leave your stuff in the compulsory cloakroom will cost you the price of a pint back home. Those younger than 20 may have difficulty gaining entry to many clubs but it helps to carry ID.

Naturally, this city of over half a million also has more sedate forms of entertainment. Jazz is relatively big and, in summer, jazz fans might be fortunate enough to catch the jazz festival in late August. There are also regular live sessions at Gothenburg's **Nefertiti** (see page 73) and **Jazzå** (see page 85) clubs. The **Konserthuset** hosts regular classical music concerts given by the Gothenburg Symphony Orchestra, which specialises in a wide-ranging Nordic repertoire. If you do go to the opera, be aware that the subtitles will be in Swedish.

● *Party at one of the city's clubs*

This is, of course, no great disaster, especially if you're familiar with the story.

Cinema is also an option for non-Swedes, as no films are dubbed into Swedish for the silver screen, except those for very young children. These are screened in one original and one dubbed version. There are 38 cinema screens across the city so you should have few problems tracking down a film you fancy seeing. Try these establishments:

Biopalatset ⓐ Kungstorget 2 ⓣ 085 626 00 00 ⓦ www.sf.se

Filmstaden ⓐ Kungsgatan 35 ⓣ 085 626 00 00

Hagabion ⓐ Linnégatan 21 ⓣ 031 42 88 10 ⓦ www.hagabion.nu

Swedish theatre obviously presents the same linguistic challenges as a trip to the opera. However, all is not lost, as the **Gothenburg English Speaking Theatre** (GEST ⓦ www.gest.se) performs plays in their original language at the Hagateatern. Their productions are few and far between, though there is demand for English-language theatre in Gothenburg from the many expats who have settled here.

○ After dark, Liseberg's Christmas lights will draw you in

Sport & relaxation

As many a football, ice-hockey and athletics fan knows, the Swedes are sports fanatics and take great pleasure in giving the rest of the world a good thrashing whenever possible. Their prowess at a wide range of sports may be down, in no small part, to the excellent facilities they have at their disposal.

Tourists usually engage in a number of activities in and around Gothenburg, such as cycling, watersports and golf. There are several cycle-hire centres in the city and pedal power can be an enjoyable way of seeing the sights. You certainly won't be alone on the comprehensive system of cycle tracks that riddle the city centre and beyond. To the north and south of the city there are some superb places for swimming, diving and windsurfing or just lounging around on a beach. Golfers have a whopping 30 courses to choose from in the greater Gothenburg area, the biggest at Öijared, boasting 63 holes. If this all seems too strenuous, you can always retreat to Haga Spa (see page 78) for a bit of pampering or just go for a relaxing swim in one of the pools.

SPECTATOR SPORTS

The 'name of the game' in Gothenburg, and indeed across the country, is ice hockey. The local team, the Frölunda Indians, play their matches at the Scandinavium ice-hockey stadium every week during the season, and you will certainly notice the symbol of the team, an Indian's head, plastered around the city. Matches are followed with passion at the stadium as well as in pubs and bars across Gothenburg.

The IFK Göteborg football team has found a new home at the Nya Gamla Ullevi stadium. The mighty IFK dominated Swedish football in the 1990s with their positively Viking style of play, and their greatest moments on the European scene so far have been winning the UEFA cup in 1982 and again in 1987.

○ *Catch a game of ice hockey with Gothenburg's local team, the Frölunda Indians*

Accommodation

Gothenburg has ample accommodation to suit every extreme of pocket and taste. Even those looking for bargain-basement hostels are well catered for. The tourist office can book accommodation for a fee of SEK 60 and booking ahead is advisable, as you never know what major event the city may be holding at the time. In summer, the tourist office can also arrange private rooms for about two-thirds of the price of three-star hotel accommodation.

HOTELS

Hotel Aveny Turist £ This small, 14-room budget hotel off the Avenyn is a good place to stay if you want to be near the centre of gravity of Gothenburg's nightlife. Rooms are surprisingly well furnished and comfortable, despite the low price tag by Swedish standards. ❷ Södra Vägen 2 (Inom Vallgraven) ❶ 031 20 52 86

Hotel Robinson £–££ Situated amid a cluster of hotels on Hotel Square, near the Nordstan shopping centre and Central Station, this is the least expensive of the bunch here, with the lowest standards but a good fall-back option. Rooms range from semi-

PRICE CATEGORIES
Average price for a room for two:
£ up to SEK 750 **££** SEK 750–1,500 **£££** over SEK 1,500

luxury with en-suite facilities to cheap and cheerful basic with shared toilet and bathroom. Noise can be an issue here.
ⓐ Södra Hamngatan 2 (Inom Vallgraven) ⓣ 031 80 25 21
ⓦ www.hotelrobinson.se

Hotel Vasa ££ The 48-room Vasa can be found in Vasastan, near the university. Rooms are light and airy and there is a sunny patio where you can enjoy your breakfast. The hotel also has a dedicated relaxation area. ⓐ Viktoriagatan 6 (Vasastan)
ⓣ 031 17 36 30 ⓦ www.hotelvasa.se

Hotell Barken Viking ££ Fancy staying on a hundred-year-old ship, a stone's throw from the city centre? The *Barken Viking*, built in 1906 in Copenhagen and moored at Gothenburg harbour, contains crew quarters with bunk beds and shared facilities, as well as relatively spacious en-suite officers' cabins. Apparently the ship doesn't bob up and down too much, so seasickness shouldn't be a problem. ⓐ Gullbergskajen (Inom Vallgraven) ⓣ 031 63 58 00 ⓦ www.liseberg.com

Hotel Eggers ££–£££ The grand building of the Hotel Eggers is conveniently located near the Brunnsparken tram interchange, the Nordstan centre and the coach and railway stations. It's one of the oldest hotels in all Sweden still in operation and is dripping with old-world charm. It's not cheap, but the location and character are worth it. Rooms are immaculate and the service impeccable. ⓐ Drottningtorget (Inom Vallgraven)
ⓣ 031 333 44 40 ⓦ www.hoteleggers.se

Elite Plaza £££ Located slap bang in the centre of the Inom Vallgraven, this is possibly Gothenburg's top five-star hotel, with rates to match. The spacious rooms in this late 19th-century building are elegant and understated, and a night's sleep in one will set you back up to SEK 2,000. ⓐ Västra Hamngatan 3 (Inom Vallgraven) ⓣ 031 720 40 00 ⓦ www.elite.se

Gothia Towers £££ The name of this four-star hotel sounds as though it belongs to a haunted medieval castle inhabited by vampires. In reality this is one of Gothenburg's most modern business hotels – and the biggest in the Nordic region, with more than 700 rooms. ⓐ Mässans Gata 24 (Vasastan) ⓣ 031 750 88 00 ⓦ www.gothiatowers.com

APARTMENTS

SGS Veckobostäder £ The SGS Veckobostäder Company, based just to the south of the Liseberg Amusement Park, has well-equipped rooms in apartments to let for around the same as a night in a three-star hotel. This sort of accommodation lends itself to longer stays, but the agency will rent you a room for just one night, if you so wish. ⓐ Utlandagatan 24 (Vasastan) ⓣ 031 333 63 90 ⓦ www.sgsveckobostader.se

HOSTELS

Göteborgs Mini-Hotel £ Situated in a quiet street in the Linné district, this hostel-cum-hotel is a welcoming place with friendly staff and a pleasant atmosphere. The price per bed does not include sheets or breakfast. It's popular, so booking ahead even in winter

The sleek exterior of the Gothia Towers

may be a good idea. ⓐ Tredje Långgatan 31 (Haga & Linné)
ⓣ 031 24 10 23 ⓦ www.minihotel.se

Masthuggsterrassens Vandrarhem £ *Vandrarhem* means youth
hostel in Swedish. The Masthuggsterrassens is affiliated to the
SVIF (Sveriges Vandrarhem i Förening/Swedish Youth Hostel
Association). Situated a short tram ride from the city centre, this
is a spotless, friendly, well-run place and good value for money.
ⓐ Masthuggsterrassen 10 (Haga & Linné) ⓣ 031 42 48 20
ⓦ www.mastenvandrarhem.com ⓥ Tram: 3, 9, 11 (Masthuggstorget)

CAMPSITES

Kärralund £ Owned by the Liseberg Amusement Park, this is the
closest campsite to the city centre, which can be reached easily
by tram. Open year-round, there is ample space for pitching tents,
as well as numerous cosy log cabins. The campsite is geared
towards families with children, though everyone is welcome.
ⓐ Olbersgatan 9 (Inom Vallgraven) ⓣ 031 84 02 00
ⓦ www.liseberg.com ⓥ Tram: 5 (Welandergatan)

THE BEST OF GOTHENBURG

Whether you are spending a half-day in the city en route to somewhere else or enjoying a full-blown holiday here, there are certain sights, places and experiences that just shouldn't be missed.

TOP 10 ATTRACTIONS

- **Avenyn** Strike a pose on one of Sweden's most fashionable boulevards (see page 90).

- **City tour on a Paddan boat** See Gothenburg from a watery perspective (see page 58).

- **Slottsskogen** Pack a picnic and relax among the family-friendly foliage of the city's biggest park (see page 79).

- **Botanical Gardens** Yes, plants can grow without sunlight for six months of the year, so watch out for falling fruit (see page 79).

- **City-centre shopping** Money, Money, Money – shop till you drop in the retail capital of northern Europe (see page 22).

Göteborgs-Posten   PADDAN

- **Gothia Towers & Lipstick Tower** Get a bird's-eye view of the city from either of these lofty lookouts (see pages 37 & 62).

- **People-watching & meandering in Haga** Mingle with the hip and cool residents of this (once condemned) now flourishing quarter and immerse yourself in the café culture (see page 74).

- **Liseberg Amusement Park** Scandinavia's biggest and best amusement park – around three million visitors a year can't be wrong (see page 91).

- **Konstmuseum** The world's finest collection of Nordic art (see page 92).

- **Maritiman** The world's largest floating museum (see page 62).

⬤ *The Lipstick Tower overlooks the Göta River*

Suggested itineraries

HALF-DAY: GOTHENBURG IN A HURRY

Half a day won't see you kicking back with a latte in a street café or wandering the cobbled lanes of Haga, but it is just sufficient

● *Enjoy some public art on the Avenyn*

time to manage either the City Museum or Maritime Centre and take a stroll up the Avenyn to call on Poseidon.

1 DAY: TIME TO SEE A LITTLE MORE

Start the day with breakfast at SoHo then take a tour of the city on a Paddan boat. You may fit in a visit to the City Museum before ending the morning at the Kronhuset in the Inom Vallgraven with a traditional lunch at the Café Kronhuset. In the afternoon join the crowds on the Avenyn, from where you should gravitate slowly through Vasastan towards the Liseberg Amusement Park for a few rides. End the day at one of the city's superb restaurants for some local seafood.

2–3 DAYS: TIME TO SEE MUCH MORE

Having two days at your disposal means you will be lucky enough to see all the major sights in the Inom Vallgraven, the harbour and around the Avenyn as well as venturing into the tightly packed streets of Haga and Linné to enjoy some of the city's famous café culture. A third day could be spent exploring one of the fortresses at either Kungälv to the north or Varberg to the south. You could even hire a car and make a day trip to Marstrand and the Bohuslän Coast.

LONGER: ENJOYING GOTHENBURG TO THE FULL

From the harbour to Linné and the Inom Vallgraven to the Liseberg Amusement Park, Gothenburg can be done in full in a week, with time enough to perhaps stay overnight in Varberg or Kungälv, for a little variety. Using the city as a base, you could even spare a few days to explore the beautiful Bohuslän Coast in more detail.

Something for nothing

Freebies are not exactly in great abundance in Sweden's second city. Not a single one of the city's museums has a day when admission is free – although you will gain free entrance to all of them when you brandish your **Gothenburg Pass** (see page 134) – and the vast majority of visitor activities require a permanent fuel line to your bank account. Even the tourist office isn't overgenerous with its handouts, and you may just have to resign yourself to the fact that, in Sweden, you get what you pay for, and pay for what you get.

Most of what Gothenburg has to offer for the financially challenged will only cost you a bit of legwork and shoe leather. The best things in life usually *don't* involve a credit card, and this is particularly true of the city's wealth of parks and green areas. The Vasaparken, the Skansparken, the Slottsskogen and the tree-lined canal banks can all be accessed without an öre to your name. Wandering the gentrified streets of Haga won't cost you a vegetarian sausage and, of course, it's perfectly possible to admire the architectural beauty of many monuments for free – by staying on the outside! The city's indoor markets can all be visited free of charge, the best of these being Gothenburg's temple to seafood, the Feskekôrka.

If you are lucky enough to be under 25, however, a whole host of museums offer free entry, including the Röhsska Museum of Fashion, Design and Decorative Arts and the Gothenburg Museum of Art (Göteborgs Konstmuseum), awarded three stars in the Michelin Green Guide, where visitors can see the world's foremost collection of Nordic art. The Museum of Natural History

(Göteborgs Naturhistoriska museum) offers the same deal. Perhaps the biggest freebie of the year comes in the form of the Kulturkalaset or Culture Festival (see page 12). The bulk of events held on the city's streets, including street theatre and concerts, are a great way of enjoying the city without spending a krona.

◉ *Green spaces are free for all to enjoy*

When it rains

When the heavens open (and they often do in this part of the world), or when the wind drives the snow so hard it never touches the ground, Gothenburg has plenty of walled and roofed spaces where benumbed and soggy visitors can seek refuge. When the drizzly half-light of a Nordic winter descends, or a summer electric storm threatens, this is a good time to take to the shops. The Nordstan (see page 67) is big enough for you to spend days inside and never have to emerge from beneath the artificial lighting, and the same is true of the other shopping malls across the street along Fredsgatan. The big three indoor markets – the Stora Saluhallen, the Feskekôrka and the Saluhall Briggen – are all atmospheric places when raindrops drum on their roofs.

Inclement weather provides the perfect excuse to dive into one of Gothenburg's countless cafés for a caffeine and sugar fix. If this seems like too idle a pastime, why not make full use of that Gothenburg Pass in your back pocket and explore some of the city's fine museums? A visit to the City Museum, the Universeum, the Museum of World Culture or the Röhsska Design Museum will outlast any summer shower, and the ideal choice on the Avenyn is the superb City Art Museum (Konstmuseum). If you're not in the mood for highbrow distractions, why not climb the Lipstick Tower or visit the café at the Gothia Towers Hotel and watch the city get a soaking from above? One way to stay out of the rain but get wet at the same time is to pay a visit to Haga Spa on Södra Allégatan. You could also lose yourself amid a jungle of tropical plants in the palm house in Trädgårdsföreningen Park.

⬥ *Shelter from the rain inside the Nordstan shopping centre*

On arrival

TIME DIFFERENCE

Gothenburg, and indeed the whole of Sweden, is in a time zone one hour ahead of Greenwich Mean Time. The clocks go forward one hour for daylight saving in March, and back again in October.

ARRIVING

By air

Unless you're travelling with Ryanair, your flight will touch down at Gothenburg's Landvetter Airport, some 25 km (15½ miles) west of the city centre. Having passed smoothly through passport control and customs, you emerge into the cavernous modern hall of the airport where there are several cash machines and a Forex exchange office. To reach the city centre, board one of the Flygbussarna express coaches, which leave around every 20 minutes from outside departures (tickets from the driver, SEK 80 for a single, debit and credit cards accepted). The specially adapted buses with spacious luggage racks will drop you off at either the Kungsportsavenyn, the Kungsportsplatsen or the Nils Ericson Coach Station, where the service terminates. The journey takes no more than 40 minutes. If you are travelling no-frills-style with Ryanair, you'll actually arrive closer to central Gothenburg, at Göteborg City Airport, from where the same coach company will transport you the 15 km (9½ miles) to the Nils Ericson Coach Station in 30 minutes for SEK 60.

By rail

All train services terminate at Gothenburg's Central Station.

By road

National, international and local bus services all terminate at the Nils Ericson Coach Station behind the railway station. The two buildings have been welded together to form one large and convenient public transport interchange.

🔺 *The Central Station is the hub for most forms of public transport*

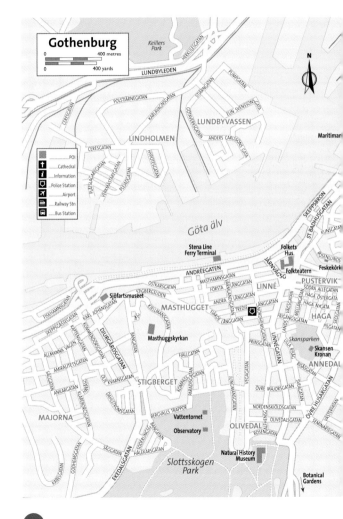

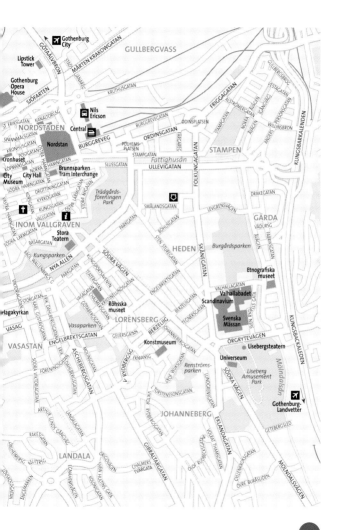

FINDING YOUR FEET

After sorting out a place to lay your head at night, your first port of call should be a branch of Gothenburg's tourist office (see page 134), where the amiable and welcoming staff will supply you with a detailed city map.

Gothenburg is, in general, a safe city, and crime against foreigners is very rare indeed. Public drunkenness is not common, but there is a tendency for large groups to become rowdy and aggressive when inebriated, so steer clear of them if possible. In Gothenburg, pedestrians, cars, bikes and trams each have their own strip of the street they can use, so make sure you're on the right one. Most visitors have a close shave with a bike or tram sooner or later.

ORIENTATION

The city centre is more spread out than the tourist information would have you believe. It is divided into three distinct areas: the Inom Vallgraven is the old historic core bordered by canals on three sides and the sea on the other. Here you will find the main historical sights, the harbour, bus and railway stations and the best shopping areas. This is the busiest part of town, with trams wending their way across the cobbles, and cafés, restaurants and pubs spilling out on to the streets in summer and enticing passers-by with their cosy interiors in winter. The second district, to the south, is Vasastan, the area around Gothenburg's main thoroughfare, the Kungsportsavenyn (generally snipped to just Avenyn). The streets around here abound in 19th-century architecture, while the Avenyn itself is a bold, sweeping boulevard that glides its way confidently from the Kungsportsplatsen 1 km

IF YOU GET LOST, TRY ...

Do you speak English?
Talar ni engelska?
Taalar nee engelska?

Where is ...?
Var ligger ...?
Vaar ligger ...?

Could you show me where I am on the map?
Kan ni visa på kartan var jag är?
Kun nee veesa paw kaartan vaar yaag air?

(½ mile) up to the Götaplatsen. Haga and Linné to the west of
Vasastan constitute the final area – Haga is the old working-
class district, now a trendy address packed with craft shops and
toasty cafés. Some of Linné has kept a smidgen of its hard-knock
dockworker image.

GETTING AROUND

Gothenburg must have one of the most efficient and user-friendly
public transport systems in Europe, with blue trams, buses and
ferries whisking you anywhere you care to go in the city and
beyond. As a tourist, you are unlikely to use the city's buses much,
apart from the Green Express up to Kungälv perhaps, but central
Gothenburg is spread out enough to warrant using the trams.
Unless you have a Gothenburg Pass, you'll have to acquire a ticket.
All things considered, it's probably best to opt for single tickets,
which cost a minimum of SEK 25 from the driver. You can also
buy tickets via SMS. Check the postings at the stop for the code

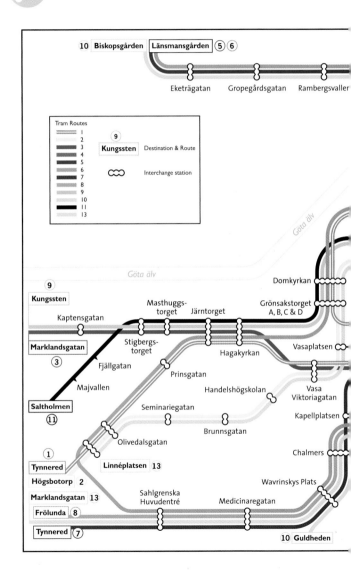

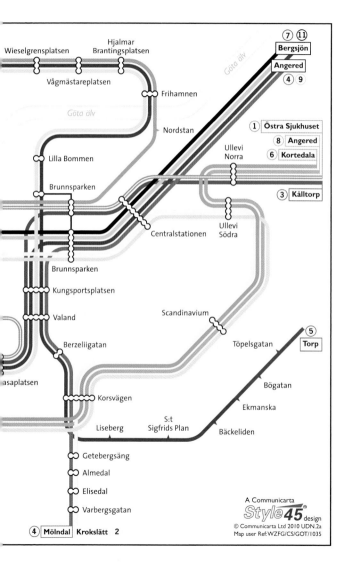

for the ticket you want. Remember to stamp your ticket in the machines inside the vehicle otherwise you will be liable to pay a hefty fine if caught. Saying you're a foreigner and that you bought a ticket will cut no ice whatsoever with the inspectors.

The well-ordered system is operated by **Västtrafik** (ⓦ www.vasttrafik.se), which has a ticket and information office at Brunnsparken tram stop C.

Car hire

Gothenburg has one of the best public transport systems you're likely to ride anywhere in Europe, so hiring a car may be a luxury you can do without. You may, however, want to equip yourself with your own set of wheels for the 80-km (50-mile) trip south to Varberg or to explore the Bohuslän Coast. Driving in Sweden is a joy, with road surfaces like billiard tables, clear road signs and markings and generally courteous fellow road-users.

These are the best car-rental companies to try, and don't forget that it's often cheaper to book in advance through your airline's affiliate.

Avis ⓐ Landvetter Airport ⓣ 031 94 73 30 ⓦ www.avis.se
Hertz ⓐ Landvetter Airport ⓣ 031 94 60 20 ⓦ www.hertz.se
Mabi Hyrbilar ⓐ Kilsgatan 5 ⓣ 031 774 97 00 ⓦ www.mabihyrbilar.se

ⓞ *Gothenburg city centre on a summer's evening*

THE CITY OF
Gothenburg

Inom Vallgraven

Locked within a watery ring of canals and sea, the Inom Vallgraven is the oldest part of town, containing most of Gothenburg's oldest historic sites. This is the site of the original city founded by Gustav Adolf II in 1621 and the place most visitors embark on their exploration of the city's sights. The Inom Vallgraven is an area of wide, spacious squares and narrow, pedestrianised cobbled streets, a stark contrast to the grand, wide boulevards dating from the 19th century elsewhere in the city. The Inom Vallgraven is where Gothenburg's best indoor shopping can be had, as well as some of the best pubs and restaurants. You're unlikely to need the services of the city's excellent public transport system here and, indeed, getting around on foot is your only option in much of this part of town.

A novel way to tour at least the perimeter of the Inom Vallgraven in summer is to take a **Paddan boat cruise** (ⓦ www.paddan.com). These long, open barges with bench-type seats take 50 minutes to negotiate a circular route from the Kungsportsbron at the end of the Avenyn, west along the Rosenlunds Canal, past the Feskekôrka, out into the harbour and north as far as the Götaälvbron and back inland via the Stora Hamn Canal to the starting point. There are sailings almost every 15 minutes, and every boat comes with a guide who will point out interesting features and outline the history and development of the city. 'Cheerful yellow ponchos', to quote the website, are provided when it rains (as it fairly frequently does).

Vintage tram rides are another take on the classic city tour
(Ⓦ www.ringlinien.org). These run daily in July and August and
at weekends in spring and autumn. Ask at the tourist office for
routes and tickets.

SIGHTS & ATTRACTIONS

Gothenburg Cathedral

Gothenburg's rather unassuming cathedral just off Kungsgatan
stands on the site of a church built here at the same time as the
city was established, in 1621. In 1633 it was dedicated to the city's
founder, who fell in the Battle of Lützen a year earlier, and ever
since it has been known as 'Gustav's Cathedral'. Destroyed on
several occasions in blazes, the building we see today is the third
to grace the pretty square. The modest, light, neoclassical interior
occasionally echoes to the tones of church music concerts
and choir recitals. Ⓦ www.svenskakyrkan.se Ⓛ 08.00–18.00
Mon–Fri, 09.00–16.00 Sat, 10.00–15.00 Sun

Gustav Adolfs Torg & around

Gothenburg's largest square straddles the Stora Hamn Canal
and is the site of some of the city's most grandiose and important
buildings. In the middle rises a statue of a dashing Gustav Adolf
II pointing to the spot where he proclaimed 'Here I will build my
city', which he duly did. Along the northern edge of the square
stand two sturdy palaces belonging to the City Hall (Rådhus)
and the Stock Exchange (Börsen). Next door to the City Hall is
the so-called German Church dating from 1748, whose tower
dominates the skyline of the old quarter.

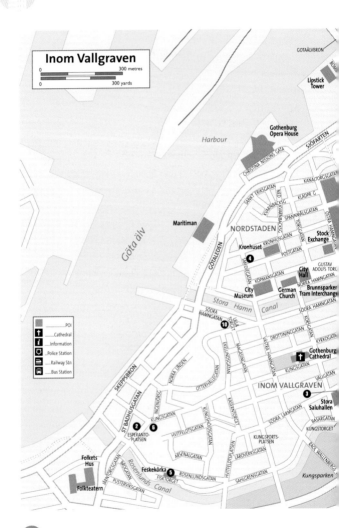

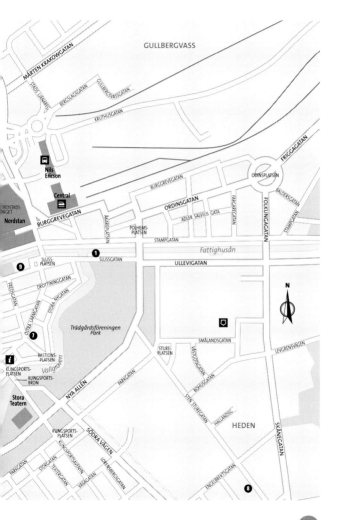

Harbour area

Gothenburg's harbour, to the north of the Inom Vallgraven, is home to some of the city's most distinctive sights, albeit not always from architecture's top draw. Starting at the southern end, **Maritiman** (Gothenburg's Maritime Centre) claims to be the biggest floating ship museum in the world. The 19 ships, boats and barges are paradise for anyone who has a penchant for things that bob on water, have sails and are inhabited by seamen, and the exhibits are an 'all hands on deck' kind of experience.

Heading further north you will soon arrive at the **Gothenburg Opera House**, which is unlike any other opera house you're likely to come across anywhere else. Its ground-breaking maritime-style architecture makes the harbour building resemble an imposing ship. The architect, Jan Izkowitz, strived to make it feel 'possessed by an airiness that sends your mind soaring across the meandering landscape like wings of seagulls'. The result, inaugurated in 1994, is both poetic and brutal at the same time. The **Lipstick Tower** is located further north along the Göta River at Barken Viking. Built by British-Swedish architect Ralph Erskine (creator of the innovative, eco-friendly Greenwich Millennium Village in London) in the 1980s, the skyscraper gets its name from the fact that it looks uncannily like a used red lipstick. A lift elevates visitors to the 22nd floor, from where there are fantastic views back across the city, as well as a café.

Lipstick Tower ⓐ Lilla Bommen ⓛ 11.00–16.00 (June–Aug); 11.00–16.00 Mon–Fri (Sept–May) ⓘ Admission charge

Maritiman (Maritime Centre) ⓐ Packhuskajen 8 ⓣ 031 10 59 50 ⓦ www.maritiman.se ⓛ 10.00–16.00 Fri–Sun (Mar & Nov); 10.00–16.00 Apr, May & Oct; 10.00–18.00 (June–Sept) ⓝ Tram: 5, 10 (Lilla Bommen) ⓘ Admission charge

⬥ *The Kronhuset is the city's oldest building*

Kronhuset

Built between 1642 and 1654 by the Dutch as an artillery store, the Kronhuset is Gothenburg's oldest building. Hidden behind the walls of a cobbled enclosure, its red brick façades and greenish metal shutters really do look ancient in this city of 19th-century grandeur and 20th-century Art Nouveau and functionalism. One of the best times to visit is December when the interior is jam-packed with stalls selling traditional Swedish yuletide craft items. Expensive craft shops fill the building of the Kronhusbodarna, which lines the courtyard outside, and this is also home to one of the old quarter's most authentic eateries.
ⓐ Postgatan 6–8 ⓦ www.kronhusbodarna.nu

Kungstorget & Kungsportsplatsen

These two squares sit side by side at the southern flank of the Inom Vallgraven. Kungsportsplatsen is many tourists' starting point, as here you will find the main tourist office on the corner near the tram stop. The Kungsportsplatsen stop is also important as you can hop on buses to the airport and Kungälv here, as well as trams to the Avenyn and farther afield.

A few steps from the tourist office door stands the so-called 'Copper Mare'. A favourite activity among recent arrivals to the city is checking whether this is actually a mare (it isn't). The green statue is given a ghoulish appearance with green illumination at night.

Many mistake the large building filling the Kungstorget for the railway station. Despite looking like a Victorian rail terminal, the **Stora Saluhallen**, built in 1888, houses a wonderful indoor market with stalls selling meat, fruit and veg, cheese and various other more exotic foodstuffs. It is peppered with tiny cafés, snack

◔ The Trädgårdsföreningen resembles London's former Crystal Palace

bars and counter eateries and is one of the best places in the city centre to grab a quick plate of something tasty or put together the ingredients for a picnic to eat in one of the nearby parks along the canal banks.

Trädgårdsföreningen Park

This pretty, green expanse just to the east of the Kungsportsplatsen was founded as a central park in 1842. It is home to a wonderful rosarium and an elegant palm house, bolted together in 1878 and containing hundreds of tropical trees and shrubs. It is said to be a copy of London's Crystal Palace. ☎ 031 365 58 58 ⓦ www.tradgardsforeningen.se 🕓 10.00–20.00 (July–Sept); 07.00–18.00 (Oct–June) (phone or check website in advance as hours are subject to change) ❶ Admission charge

CULTURE

City Museum

A few steps west from the German Church brings you to the brick edifice of one of Gothenburg's most distinguished structures – the former Swedish East India Company headquarters, now home to the Gothenburg City Museum. Inside you'll find lively exhibitions on the history of the East India Company, Gothenburg's industrial history and an interesting section dedicated to life in the 1950s, as well as the wonderful period interiors of the building itself. ⓐ Norra Hamngatan 12 ☎ 031 368 36 00 ⓦ www.stadsmuseum.goteborg.se 🕓 10.00–17.00 Tues & Thur–Sun, 10.00–20.00 Wed, closed Mon ⓝ Tram: 1, 6, 9, 11 (Domkyrkan) ❶ Admission charge (free to under-25s)

RETAIL THERAPY

Fredsgatan Across the road from the Nordstan (see below) are several other large shopping centres that run the length of Fredsgatan. The Arkaden, Citypassagen and Kompassen centres all merge into one to form a kind of Nordstan B. The shops here tend to be slightly more exclusive than in the Nordstan.

Kungsgatan Another great shopping precinct is the main pedestrianised drag through the Inom Vallgraven, running east to west from the Fredsgatan almost to the sea. Here you'll find hundreds of shops, though there are more Swedish brands than international chains.

Nordstan This vast indoor shopping mall occupying several blocks between Brunnsparken and the harbour area is Scandinavia's largest. It may be looking its age a bit from the outside, but inside it's as modern and gleaming as ever and always packed full of shopaholics on a binge. The Nordstan is so vast it boasts 150 retail outlets and no fewer than three branches of McDonald's. You could come to Gothenburg and literally spend your entire city break going from shop to shop. Some probably do.
ⓐ Nordstadstorget ⓣ 031 700 86 60 ⓦ www.nordstan.se
ⓛ 10.00–19.00 Mon–Fri, 10.00–18.00 Sat, 11.00–17.00 Sun

TAKING A BREAK

Rosenkaféet £ ❶ The 'Rose Café' is the loveliest café in town, treasured by both the youngest and the oldest Gothenburgers.

In summer, Trädgårdsföreningen's café is surrounded by lush greenery. This little oasis offers dessert pies, cakes, sandwiches and light meals. ⓐ Slussgatan 1, Trädgårdsföreningen ⓣ 031 80 29 70 ⓦ www.rosenkafeet.se ⓛ 11.00–16.00 Mon–Fri, 11.00–17.00 Sat & Sun (May); 11.00–18.00 Mon–Fri, 11.00–19.00 Sat & Sun (June); 11.00–20.00 (July–Sept); closed Oct–Apr

Språkcaféet £ ❷ The 'Language Café' on fittingly named Esperanto Square is a little off the beaten track but is worth the hike up Kungsgatan for the superb range of cakes and hot and cold sandwiches they serve or for the vegetarian lunch buffet. By day this is a laid-back café with a wooden floor, book-lined walls and a vaulted ceiling. In the evening tables are pushed together and the flags of various nations placed around the dining room transform it into a place people can come and practise speaking a host of foreign tongues over a coffee or two. ⓐ Esperantoplatsen 7–9 ⓣ 031 774 21 50 ⓦ www.sprakcafeet.com ⓛ 08.00–20.00 Mon–Thur, 08.00–17.30 Fri, 10.00–17.30 Sat, closed Sun ⓝ Tram: 3, 6, 9, 11 (Järntorget)

Stora Saluhallen £ ❸ Gothenburg's largest indoor market has more than 40 stalls and small eateries and is a convenient spot for a light lunch, mid-morning snack or just an aromatic wander. ⓐ Kungstorget ⓣ 031 711 78 78 ⓛ 09.00–18.00 Mon–Fri, 09.00–15.00 Sat, closed Sun

Café Kronhuset £–££ ❹ Affordable, traditional food, a blazing log fire in winter, a cosy dining area with lots of small tables bunched together and a lively atmosphere all come together to

🔻 The Stora Saluhallen market offers the best in Swedish produce

make this one of the best places to have lunch in the old quarter.
ⓐ Postgatan 6–8 ⓣ 031 711 08 32 ⓦ www.cafekronhuset.se
ⓛ 10.00–19.00 Mon–Fri, 11.00–18.00 Sat & Sun

Feskekôrka £–££ ❺ Gothenburg's famous church-like fish market
houses two small seafood eateries, one upstairs, one downstairs.
ⓐ Fisktorget ⓛ 09.00–17.00 Tues–Thur, 09.00–18.00 Fri,
10.00–15.00 Sat, closed Sun & Mon

Södra Liden £–££ ❻ This small restaurant-cum-bar at the
unfashionable end of Kungsgatan serves a mix of pastas,
meat and fish dishes in a lively dining area or on the roof
terrace. ⓐ Kungsgatan 8 ⓣ 031 13 15 12 ⓛ Hours vary

AFTER DARK

RESTAURANTS

SoHo £–££ ❼ SoHo is a one-stop shop for all your eating and
drinking needs. Start the day with a healthy breakfast
downstairs, at midday enjoy their buffet lunch, drop in around
16.00 for coffee and cakes and round off the day with dinner
and a few cocktails. This is one of the most welcoming places
in town, with a dining area, bar, library and even a beanbag
area with low tables, all spread out over two spacious floors.
The location near the tourist office is also a big plus, and be
sure not to miss their Saturday jazz nights. ⓐ Östra Larmgatan 16
ⓣ 031 13 33 26 ⓦ www.sohogothenburg.se ⓛ 08.00–23.00
Mon–Thur, 08.00–01.00 Fri, 10.00–01.00 Sat, 11.30–17.00 Sun
(open later on club nights)

Trattoria da Pasquale £–££ ❽ An authentic Italian restaurant, with checked red and white tablecloths, candles and wonderful food. Prices are surprisingly low and the trattoria can get pretty crowded. ⓐ Sten Sturegatan 17 ⓣ 031 16 42 16 ⓛ 11.30–22.00 Mon–Fri, 13.00–22.00 Sat & Sun

Palace ££–£££ ❾ If it's old-world charm you're seeking, look no further than the Palace near the Brunnsparken tram interchange. This full-blown restaurant is something special, and just the setting for a candlelit dinner or perhaps just a few pleasant drinks with a date at the huge, zinc-topped bar. The elegantly laid tables, scurrying waitresses and rococo flourishes to the décor all add to its charm. ⓐ Södra Hamngatan 2 ⓣ 031 80 75 50 ⓦ www.palace.se ⓛ 11.30–24.00 Mon–Wed, 11.30–03.00 Thur & Fri, 12.00–03.00 Sat, 13.00–20.00 Sun

Fiskekrogen £££ ❿ This is one of Gothenburg's more upmarket fish restaurants, with prices to match. The 'Fish Tavern', as the name translates, is housed in the 19th-century Board of Trade House and has a wonderfully stylish dining area. A great place to take someone you want to impress. ⓐ Lilla Torget 1 ⓣ 031 10 10 05 ⓦ www.fiskekrogen.com ⓛ 11.30–14.00, 17.30–late Mon–Fri, 13.00–late Sat, closed Sun

BARS & CLUBS

7: ans ölhall This spit-and-sawdust miniature beer hall opposite the Saluhallen market is one of the most atmospheric and authentic places to enjoy some *öl* (beer) in town. It's been here for over 100 years and doesn't seem to have changed much over

◯ One of many ways to spend time, relaxing at a café

that time. Enjoy a boozy session (but no food) around tables displaying a century's worth of ale stains and scratches, while watching Sweden beat the rest of the world at ice hockey on the enormous TV screen. Rowdy but fun. ⓐ Kungstorget 7 ⓣ 031 13 60 79 ⓛ 10.00–24.00 Mon–Thur, 11.00–01.00 Fri & Sat, closed Sun

The Dubliner This conveniently located mock Irish tavern is a firm favourite with expats. The Dubliner is like a kitsch Swedish version of an Irish pub. Expect lots of dark wood, spilt beer, a raucous atmosphere and live music most nights. ⓐ Östra Hamngatan 50B ⓣ 031 13 90 20 ⓦ www.dubliner.se ⓛ 11.00–03.00. It also has a 'sister' at ⓐ Järntorget 7 ⓣ 031 12 70 32

Nefertiti Jazz fans should head straight for the Nefertiti, Gothenburg's premier jazz and blues nightspot. The club opened in 1978 and has gained legendary status in Sweden, with gigs by local musicians as well as the international jazz elite. ⓐ Hvitfeldtsplatsen 6 ⓣ 031 711 40 76 ⓦ www.nefertiti.se ⓛ 19.00–01.00 Mon, 20.00–01.00 Tues & Thur, 21.00–03.00 Wed, 21.00–04.00 Fri & Sat, 19.00–24.00 Sun

Haga & Linné

Arguably the highlight of any visit to Gothenburg is a stroll around the charming districts of Haga and Linné. These are the former working-class districts of the city, condemned to demolition in the 1980s, but now lively, bustling and attractive neighbourhoods. Once the seedy haunt of sailors, prostitutes, street-urchins, dockers and other assorted hard-knocks, the grid of tightly packed cobbled streets has been gentrified Notting Hill-style, attracting well-heeled 20- and 30-somethings, as well as the odd artist, artisan and writer. If there ever was any working-class grit in Haga, the only place you'll find it now is lodged between the cobblestones, though the place has preserved its original layout. Some streets are lined with tall 19th-century tenement blocks while further towards the Skansparken, traditional pastel-coloured timber structures can be found. Some parts of Haga away from the shopping streets have been cleaned up so much they have become a touch bland and characterless. Linné is a slightly different story as it has kept its grungy underbelly in the Långgatan series of streets just back from the Stena Line ferry terminal. Haga and Linné have some worthwhile sights, but it is the cafés and the bohemian boutiques, which cluster on every cobbled corner, that people come here to experience. If you are short on time, head straight for the most interesting thoroughfare, Haga Nygata, where most of these are found. Linnégatan, a long wide boulevard lined with tall ornate 19th-century blocks, is also an impressive sight.

⬤ *Pamper yourself at the Hagabadet Spa*

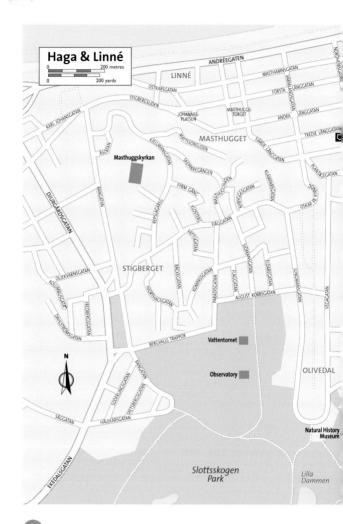

Haga & Linné

0 ————— 200 metres
0 ————— 200 yards

ANDRÉEGATEN

LINNÉ

MASTHAMNSGATAN

VÄRMLANDSGATAN

ÖSTKARSGATAN

FÖRSTA LÅNGGATAN

STIGBERGSLIDEN

ANDRA LÅNGGATAN

JOHANNES-PLATSEN

MASTHUGGS-TORGET

KARL JOHANSGATAN

TREDJE LÅNGGATAN

KJELLMANSGATAN

MATTSSONSLIDEN

MASTHUGGET

FJÄRDE LÅNGGATAN

PLANTAGEGATAN

ÅSGTAN

Masthuggskyrkan

SKEPPAREGÄNGEN

MASTHUGGSLIDEN

KLAMMARGATAN

JOSKAY PL.

OSKAR PL.

BANGATAN

FYRM GÄNG

REPSLAGARG

JURBIN

DJURGÅRDSGATAN

KLOSTERG

CARLGRENSGATAN

FJÄLLGATAN

VATTUGATAN

STIGBERGET

BACKEGATAN

KOMPASSGATAN

PARADISGATAN

SÖRHALLSGATAN

ELDAREGATAN

FLAGGATAN

OLJEKVARNSGATAN

KOLUMBUSGATAN

HÖRNTÅGSGATAN

AUGUST KOBBSGATAN

JUNGMANSGATAN

VEGAGATAN

FREDBERGSGATAN

DAHLSTRÖMSGATAN

OLIVEDAL

BERGVALLS TRAPPOR

Vattentornet

N

Observatory

SÖDERLINGSGATAN

BANGATAN

SPISTBERGSGATAN

Natural History Museum

SÄGGATAN

HÄLLEKÄRSGATAN

EKEDALSGATAN

Slottsskogen Park

Lilla Dammen

SIGHTS & ATTRACTIONS

Hagabadet

Haga Spa, located on busy Södra Allégatan, was built in the late 19th century as a bathhouse for the poor of the district. In line with the gentrification of the rest of Haga, it is now a very fine spa with a relaxing Roman bath, masseurs and Pilates classes.
ⓐ Södra Allégatan 3 ⓣ 031 60 06 00 ⓦ www.hagabadet.se
ⓛ 06.30–21.00 Mon–Thur, 06.30–20.00 Fri, 09.00–19.00 Sat, 10.00–19.00 Sun ⓝ Tram: 3, 6, 9, 11 (Hagakyrkan)
ⓘ Admission charge

Hagakyrkan

There is something pleasingly simple about Haga's parish church at the eastern end of the Haga Nygata. Built between 1856 and 1859 by an architect named Edelsvärd, the yellow brick neo-Gothic exterior gives way to a modest, dark wood and whitewashed interior. If you're lucky, you may catch an organ recital here.
ⓐ Hagaparken, a small park by Haga Kyrkogata ⓦ www.svenskakyrkan.se/haga ⓛ 11.00–15.00 Mon & Tues, 11.00–13.00 Sat, closed Sun & Wed–Fri ⓝ Tram: 3, 6, 9, 11 (Hagakyrkan)

Skansparken

To the south of Haga Nygata rises a mound of land known as the Skansparken. The principal attraction here is the Military Museum housed in a 17th-century fortress (Skansen Kronan). While the museum alone may not justify the climb up the Skansparken's steep grassy slopes, the view across Haga and beyond certainly does.

Slottsskogen Park/Canal banks

Linnégatan's wide expanse ends at Linnéplatsen, where you'll find the entrance to Gothenburg's largest park, the Slottsskogen. Gothenburg is rightly proud of the fact that there are 175 sq m (1,884 sq ft) of green space per citizen in the city. Most of that number will be made up from the Slottsskogen Park, the best place in town to join hundreds of other summertime picnickers and relax in the sun in the company of like-minded locals. The park also contains several attractions, such as a **Children's Zoo** (for information on activities for children see page 129), as well as Gothenburg's Natural History Museum, the Observatory and the city's Botanical Gardens.

The **Botanical Gardens** (ⓐ Carl Skottsbergs Gata 22A ⓣ 031 741 11 01 ⓦ www.gotbot.se ⓛ 09.00–sunset) are Sweden's largest, with more than 12,000 plant specimens and covering 175 hectares (432 acres). The Rock Garden, the Japanese Glade, the Rhododendron Valley and the glasshouses are the highlights of any visit. In 2006 Gothenburg's Botanical Gardens were declared the third most attractive gardens in Europe.

The **Slottsskogen Observatory** (ⓐ Slottsskogen ⓣ 031 12 63 00 ⓘ Admission charge) has had people seeing stars for the last 70 years. In spring, autumn and winter there are stellar shows twice a week on Mondays and Wednesdays, and in summer, when it never gets fully dark enough to see the stars, there are solar observations. Booking in advance is recommended.

The parkland along the banks of the canal on the edge of the Inom Vallgraven are also pleasant if you can escape the noise of the traffic on one side and the gawping tourists aboard the Paddan cruise boats on the other.

CULTURE

Natural History Museum

Just inside the Slottsskogen Park, the Natural History Museum is the oldest in Gothenburg and allegedly houses some ten million specimens. Away from the dusty paper-lined drawers full of insects pinned to squares of card, and frogs in formaldehyde, the most interesting exhibit here is the world's only stuffed blue whale, which, strange but true, houses a 19th-century café.
ⓐ Slottsskogen ① 031 775 24 00 ⓦ www.gnm.se ⓛ 11.00–17.00 Tues–Sun, closed Mon ⓝ Tram: 1, 6 (Linnéplatsen) ① Admission charge (free to under-25s)

RETAIL THERAPY

In contrast to the brand-name shopping of the Inom Vallgraven, Haga has more small-scale choices: craft shops, second-hand bookshops, antique emporia and design outlets are the order of the day here. Linné is less attractive, though it has a few second-hand clothes stores. ⓦ www.hagashopping.nu

TAKING A BREAK

Allégårdens Café Dickson £ ❶ A simple, cheap and cheerful coffee, cakes and sandwiches place inside the library financed by James Robertson Dickson, a Swede of Scottish heritage. ⓐ Södra Allégatan 4 ① 031 365 80 67 ⓦ www.allegarden-goteborg.se ⓛ 09.00–21.00 Mon–Thur, 09.00–15.30 Fri, closed Sat & Sun

◔ *Linné is home to some beautiful architecture*

Café Husaren £ ② Open the door of this superb café and the scent of cinnamon will wrap itself around you and draw you inside. This is where the 'Haga bun' was invented – a large cinnamon bun subsequently copied across the city. Apart from this speciality, the café also serves up a huge selection of cakes and sandwiches that you can enjoy at antique wooden tables under the fabulous ornate glass ceiling. It's the pick of the bunch in Haga Nygata, as confirmed by the signatures of illustrious visitors on the walls. ⓐ Haga Nygata 28 ① 031 13 63 78 ⓦ www.cafehusaren.se ① 09.00–20.00 Mon–Thur, 09.00–19.00 Fri, 09.00–18.00 Sat & Sun

Café Kringlan £ ③ You'll recognise the Kringlan by the huge, gold pretzel hanging above the door. Inside you encounter a tiny space packed with odd tables and chairs, the fragrance of joss sticks and the exotic lunch buffet hanging in the air and world music on the CD player. Your fellow diners are a hippy crowd enjoying chickpeas and basmati rice or students deep in thought over a book and a coffee. One of the most distinctive places on Haga Nygata, though often full. ⓐ Haga Nygata 13 ① 031 13 09 08 ① 08.00–20.00 Mon–Fri, 09.00–19.00 Sat & Sun

Cigarren £ ④ Swedes are real coffee addicts and love nothing better than a great cup of arabica or robusta. The aroma in this small café on Järntorget is fantastic, and the list of different variations on the simple cup of coffee they serve, exhaustive. Until recently this would have been enhanced by the sweet, pungent fragrance of cigar smoke as Cigarren (as the name betrays) also stocks 40 types of cigar from the Caribbean. However, since 2005 you can't smoke in cafés, so you'll be dispatched

outside to draw on your Cuban. ⓐ Järntorget 6 ⓣ 031 14 15 60
ⓛ 07.00–21.00 Mon–Fri, 10.00–21.00 Sat & Sun

Egg & Milk £ ❺ This new addition to the Gothenburg café
scene could hardly be any less Swedish. The theme is American
1950s diner, and they've gone all-out – even the waitresses are clad
accordingly in bubblegum pink dresses, aprons and little white
hats. On the calorie-packed menu: American pancakes, 12 kinds
of bagels, delicious milkshakes and omelettes. The marshmallow
latte can (thankfully) be had with just plain, Swedish milk.
ⓐ Övre Husargatan 23 ⓣ 031 701 03 50 ⓛ 07.00–15.00

Jacob's Café £ ❻ Across the road from Hemma Hos (see page 84)
stands one of the most popular cafés on Haga Nygata. Small
café tables spill out on to the cobbles in summer and inside you
can munch delicious cakes and hot sandwiches and sip superb
coffee at a jumble of tables crammed together in three rooms.
This place has one of the best atmospheres when full; it's just a
pity it's not open into the evening. ⓐ Haga Nygata 10 ⓣ 031 711
80 44 ⓛ 10.00–19.00 Mon–Sat, 11.00–19.00 Sun

Saluhall Briggen £–££ ❼ The least frequented of Gothenburg's
indoor market-cum-eateries (at least by foreign visitors) but
possibly the best. There seem to be more small diners than
stalls here, all tightly packed into a modern hall. It's the most
authentically Swedish place to lunch in Linné, with all manner
of menus. Very often the food is prepared right in front of you,
and you decide what goes into the dish. ⓐ Nordhemsgatan 28
ⓛ 09.00–18.00 Mon–Fri, 09.00–15.00 Sat, closed Sun

AFTER DARK

RESTAURANTS

Cyrano £ ❾ The small French bistro has been a local favourite for quite some time. Although it is a place for French home-style cooking, such as moules marinières and snails, strangely enough it is the pizzas that have made it so popular. The stone-oven-baked masterpieces taste like nothing else, and they are very good value. The place itself is also cute and homely, although the staff can be a little too relaxed at times. ⓐ Prinsgatan 7 ❶ 031 14 31 10 ⏰ 11.00–22.00 Mon–Fri, 14.00–22.00 Sat & Sun

Hagabions Café £ ❾ The downstairs bar in this old cinema attracts the hipster crowd, but the small restaurant upstairs is very mixed, and always pleasantly crowded with people dining before or after a movie. The menu is mainly vegetarian, yet innovative and tasty, and all the main dishes are inexpensive. Members of staff are very friendly and as a bonus they will always give you the latest scoop on what are the unmissable movies of the moment. ⓐ Linnégatan 21 ❶ 031 42 63 32 ⏰ 17.00–22.00 Mon–Fri , 13.00–22.00 Sat & Sun

Hemma Hos ££ ❿ This restaurant and bar is one of the classier places on Haga's main drag, serving up Italian, French and Swedish dishes, including seafood and even reindeer. Most people come here to eat but you could just enjoy a few drinks at the bar. The food is excellent, but prices are high. ⓐ Haga Nygata 12 ❶ 031 13 40 90 ⓦ www.hemmahos.net ⏰ 11.30–23.00 Mon–Thur, 11.30–01.00 Fri, 12.00–01.00 Sat, 12.00–21.00 Sun

Sjöbaren ££–£££ ⓫ Well designed and for the relatively well off, the trendy Sjöbaren specialises in succulent Swedish seafood. The marinated smoked salmon with dill and potatoes is a classic not to be missed. ⓐ Haga Nygata 25 ⓣ 031 711 97 80 ⓦ www.sjobaren.se ⓛ 11.00–23.00 Mon–Thur, 11.00–24.00 Fri, 12.00–24.00 Sat, 13.00–21.00 Sun

12-52 £££ ⓬ Located on the grand Linnégatan, the 12-52 bar and restaurant has an international menu with central London prices. The small, well-laid tables, the hubbub of fellow diners and the attentive waiters make this a pleasant enough place to spend the evening. ⓐ Linnégatan 52 ⓣ 031 12 52 11 ⓦ www.1252.se ⓛ 18.00–24.00 Tues–Sat, 11.30–15.00 Sun, closed Mon ⓝ Tram: 1, 6 (Olivedalsgatan)

A Hereford Beefstouw £££ ⓭ A carnivore's pleasure dome whose menu is heavy with steaks of every shape, size and weight. Order your steak, watch it being prepared by chefs in the middle of the restaurant, then pile your plate high with greens from the salad bar. ⓐ Linnégatan 5 ⓣ 031 775 04 41 ⓦ www.a-h-b.dk/goteborg ⓛ 11.30–14.00, 17.00–22.00 Mon–Fri, 16.00–22.00 Sat, 15.00–21.00 Sun ⓝ Tram: 3, 6, 9, 11 (Järntorget)

BARS & CLUBS

Jazzå One of only a few clubs in Linné, the Jazzå is one of the best jazz spots in town, with live music at least every other day. The bar is well stocked, the music top-notch, but the place slightly lacks atmosphere and character. ⓐ Andra Långgatan 4 ⓣ 031 14 16 90 ⓦ http://jazza.nu ⓛ 17.00–01.00 Sun–Thur, 17.00–02.00 Fri & Sat

Vasastan

Wander west into any street leading from the Avenyn and you will find yourself in the atmospheric streets of Vasastan (which shares its name with a more famous district of Stockholm). This is the university district, with lofty 19th-century blocks lining the streets and inexpensive cafés that fill up at mealtimes with chattering students. When night falls, the tree-lined thoroughfares, such as Vasagatan, are illuminated by the trams trundling by, and the ambience is vaguely reminiscent of pre-war Kiev or Warsaw. The wider area is home to some of Gothenburg's best-known attractions, such as the Kungsportsavenyn, the Liseberg Amusement Park, the Röhsska Museum of Design and the City Art Museum. The last in this list is just one of a cluster of buildings on Götaplatsen, including the City Theatre and the Konserthuset, which all keep watch over the most famous symbol of Gothenburg – the statue of Poseidon.

SIGHTS & ATTRACTIONS

Götaplatsen

The Avenyn's cobbled length starts at the Kungsportsplatsen and ends around 1 km (½ mile) further south at Götaplatsen, a square created to celebrate the city's 300th anniversary. The centre of the square is dominated by a large bronze statue of **Poseidon**, created by Carl Milles, Sweden's most celebrated sculptor, and installed here in 1930. The size of Poseidon's penis (deemed too large) immediately caused a kerfuffle when it was unveiled, and Milles was forced to take a chisel to the poor

🔺 *Poseidon may not look quite as you imagined when close up*

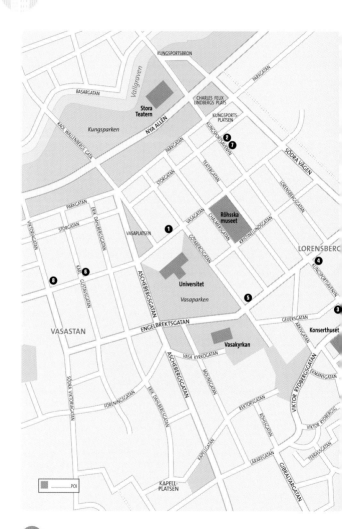

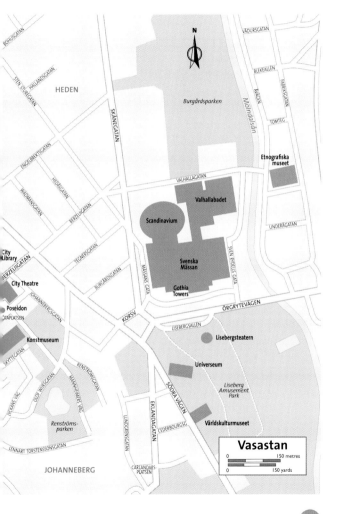

Greek god's member (judge the result for yourself). However, if you ascend the steps of the Concert Hall to the right of Poseidon, you'll see that the fish the god is holding in his right hand isn't all it seems, and that Milles probably had the last laugh when it came to Poseidon's privates. All in all, the statue isn't very aesthetically pleasing, especially the face, but despite this it has become a recognised symbol of the city.

Gothenburg's **Concert House** (Konserthuset) stands to the right of Poseidon and the City Theatre faces that across the square to the left. Note that the plays are only in Swedish and the theatre closes during the summer.

Kungsportsavenyn (Avenyn)

Somewhat understandably this mouthful of a name is shortened by the locals to Avenyn. This long boulevard plays the same role in Gothenburg as the Champs-Elysées in Paris, Wenceslas Square in Prague or La Rambla in Barcelona. Its broad, elongated space buzzes day and night with people, cars, trams, shops, bars, restaurants and nightclubs. This is Gothenburg's centre of gravity, a place to which every visitor is drawn sooner or later and a reference point for the entire city. It's the place in Gothenburg to shop, eat, drink and party, as well as partake of some of the more highbrow entertainment the city has to offer. Just strolling up and down its length you can feel the busy energy of this strip of city life. In summer, cafés spill out on to the pavements, and the 'avenue' comes alive with the Culture Festival and other events. In winter, well-dressed shoppers stroll from shop to shop, their way lit by some of the most spectacular Christmas decorations you are likely to see anywhere.

However, the Avenyn, it must be said, is also the most expensive part of an expensive city and not always the best place to eat and drink if you are on a budget (and who isn't in Sweden?). A short walk west into Vasastan proper can see prices in cafés, bars and restaurants drop by up to 50 per cent.

Liseberg Amusement Park

With around three million visitors a year and almost 40 major attractions, Liseberg is Scandinavia's number-one amusement park and one of the best in Europe. The park, just a short tram ride from the Avenyn, is a veritable riot of fairy lights, flamingo pink paintwork, screaming kids, hot-dog stands, flashing neon

One of the thrilling rides at Liseberg Amusement Park

and blaring music. Established in 1923, it isn't your typical, run-of-the-mill fun park and has a style and design you won't see anywhere else. The main draw these days is the Balder, a traditional timber roller coaster and 2 minutes 8 seconds of sheer G-force-induced hell. It's an impressive sight, even if you are too terrified to take a ride. One of the latest and scariest attractions at the park is the hair-raising Uppswinget. ⓐ Lisebergsbyn Kärralund, Olbersgatan 9 ① 031 40 01 00 ⓦ www.liseberg.com ⓛ 11.00–22.00 (May–Sept); winter hours vary, so check website for details ⓝ Tram: 4, 5, 6, 8, 13, 14 (Korsvägen) ① Admission charge

Vasaparken

Join smooching young lovers, skiving students lazing on the lawns and the odd bloke out walking his dog in the quiet park radiating out from the main university building in Vasagatan. Apart from the canal banks this is the nicest bit of greenery in Vasastan, so enjoy it when you can. ⓝ Tram: 1, 3, 7, 10 (Vasaplatsen)

CULTURE

Konstmuseum (City Art Museum)

The Götaplatsen's main attraction, and one of the highlights of a visit to Gothenburg for art fans, is the City Art Museum. Behind the stern symmetrical 1930s façade lies what is often described as the world's finest collection of Nordic art, but the gallery is also the proud owner of works by Van Gogh, Picasso, Rembrandt, Rubens and Monet. The highlights here, however, are the Fürstenburg Galleries on the sixth floor, where works by many of Scandinavia's major late 19th- and early 20th-century artists, such as Carl Larsson, Anders Zorn, Ernst Josephson, Peter Krøyer and Carl Wilhelmson, are exhibited. If you've never heard these names when you enter the museum, you'll certainly know them when you emerge again and have gained an appreciation for their work, which often depicts the Swedish countryside and scenes from rural life. ⓐ Götaplatsen ⓣ 031 368 35 00 ⓦ www.konstmuseum.goteborg.se ⓛ 11.00–18.00 Tues & Thur, 11.00–21.00 Wed, 11.00–17.00 Fri–Sun, closed Mon ⓘ Admission charge (free to under-25s)

Röhsska museet (Röhsska Museum of Fashion, Design & Decorative Arts)

Occupying one of the more historic buildings on Vasagatan is the excellent Röhsska Museum of Design, generally regarded as Sweden's finest. The 50,000 exhibits range from Greek and Roman artefacts to 1990s household objects that look as though they came out of that decade's IKEA catalogues. Most of the collections deal with Swedish and European handicrafts. A fitting museum for a nation so fascinated with innovative design. ⓐ Vasagatan 37–39 ⓣ 031 368 31 50 ⓦ www.designmuseum.se ⓛ 12.00–20.00 Tues, 12.00–17.00 Wed–Fri, 11.00–17.00 Sat & Sun, closed Mon ⓣ Tram: 3, 4, 5, 7, 10 (Valand) ⓘ Admission charge (free to under-25s and students of design, art and architecture)

Universeum (Science Museum)

This engaging museum just around the corner from the entrance to the Liseberg Amusement Park provides a fascinating experience for adults and children alike. The

huge building, with more than 3 km (2 miles) of walkways, holds sections devoted to various environments such as the rainforest, the ocean and the Swedish landscape, including numerous aquaria and mini ecosystems. Water features heavily and you may emerge slightly damper than you entered. In addition there are hands-on science exhibits, an inventor's corner (a favourite with kiddies) and much more besides.
ⓐ Södra Vägen 50 ☎ 031 335 64 50 ⓦ www.universeum.se
🕓 09.00–21.00 (summer); 10.00–18.00 (winter) Ⓣ Tram: 4, 5, 6, 8, 13, 14 (Korsvägen) ❶ Admission charge

Världskulturmuseet (Museum of World Culture)

This modern, forward-thinking museum, housed in an ultra-contemporary structure to the south of the Liseberg, exhibits interesting collections from Latin America, Africa and Asia.
ⓐ Södra Vägen 54 ☎ 031 63 27 00 ⓦ www.varldskulturmuseet.se
🕓 12.00–17.00 Tues, Fri & Sat, 12.00–21.00 Wed & Thur, closed Sun & Mon Ⓣ Tram: 4, 5, 6, 8, 13, 14 (Korsvägen)
❶ Admission charge

RETAIL THERAPY

Avenyn The place to head for in Vasastan to flex that plastic is the city's main thoroughfare. Lining the Avenyn you'll find many brand names you recognise and quite a few you don't. Shops here tend to be slightly pricier and more exclusive than those in the city's shopping malls. For a full list of shops, restaurants etc on and around the Avenyn, visit the website. ⓦ www.avenyn.se (in Swedish but decipherable)

◆ *Carl Milles' Poseidon guards the Konstmuseum*

TAKING A BREAK

Café Garbo £ ❶ Greta Garbo was actually born Greta Lovisa Gustafson in Stockholm, and the ultimate star and one of Sweden's favourite daughters is the loose theme of this basement eatery opposite the university. Enjoy affordable pastas, salads, sandwiches, coffee and cakes here. Popular with students, and often not a table to be had. ⓐ Vasagatan 40 ❶ 031 774 19 25 ⓛ 10.00–22.00 Mon–Thur, 10.00–24.00 Fri, 11.00–24.00 Sat, 11.00–22.00 Sun Ⓝ Tram: 2, 3, 7, 10, 13 (Vasaplatsen)

Condeco £ ❷ This popular chain-style trendy coffee-and-cakes joint has two other branches in Gothenburg. They also serve one of the cheapest lunch menus in the area. ⓐ Kungsportsavenyn 4 ❶ 031 711 40 10 Ⓦ www.condeco.se ⓛ 08.00–23.00 Mon–Thur, 09.00–01.00 Fri & Sat, 09.00–23.00 Sun

Junggrens Café £ ❸ Once the haunt of poor actors and artists, this old place has somehow survived. Cheap and cheerful, the friendly waitresses serve up monster-sized sandwiches, scrumptious cakes and superb coffee, which can be consumed at the window bar while watching the world go hurrying by. ⓐ Kungsportsavenyn 37 ❶ 031 16 17 51 ⓛ 08.00–22.00 Mon–Fri, 09.00–22.00 Sat & Sun

Park Aveny Café ££ ❹ It may be a little on the pricey side but it is worth it, especially in the summer when one can sit outside and enjoy watching people along Avenyn. The menu includes French classics, such as oysters, steaks and salad. The wine list is

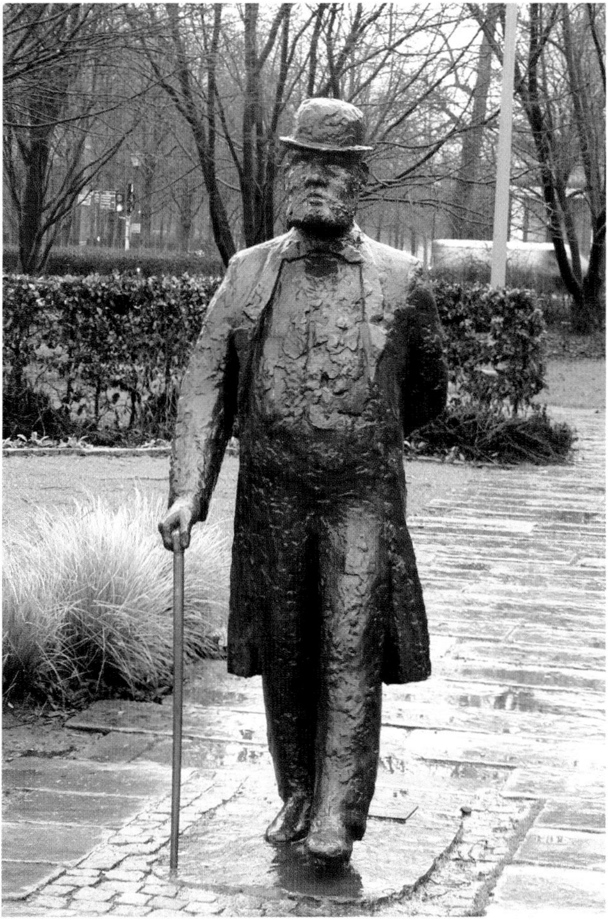

Just walking in the rain on the Avenyn

excellent. ⓐ Kungsportsavenyn 36–38 ⓣ 031 727 10 76 ⓛ 11.30–
14.00, 18.00–22.00 Mon–Fri, 17.00–22.00 Sat, 14.00–20.00 Sun

AFTER DARK

RESTAURANTS

Café Tintin £–££ ❺ Got the munchies at four in the morning?
Best head for Tintin where they serve up tasty but pricey fare
around the clock. In the early hours, and after a few drinks,
Tintin and his friends plastered surreally all over the walls and
tables may make you feel like you've had one too many.
Conveniently located just off the Avenyn. ⓐ Engelbrektsgatan 22
ⓣ 031 18 07 70 ⓛ 24 hours

Krakow £–££ ❻ This cosy Polish eatery serves up standard
stodgy eastern European fare such as *pierogi* (savoury dumplings)
and *bigos* (stew) in basic surroundings. A cheap-and-cheerful
option for a filling low-cost refuel. ⓐ Karl Gustavsgatan 28
ⓣ 031 20 33 74 ⓦ www.krakow.nu ⓛ 17.00–24.00 Mon–Thur,
17.00–01.00 Fri & Sat ⓜ Tram: 1, 3, 7, 10 (Vasaplatsen)

Brasserie Lipp ££–£££ ❼ If it's a full-blown sit-down meal or
just a few pre-club drinks you are looking for, you could do a
lot worse than Brasserie Lipp. Dine on tasty seafood, duck
and beef dishes, or take a pew at the large bar and enjoy
the chilled vibe and the company of the friendly barmen.
ⓐ Kungsportsavenyn 8 ⓣ 031 10 58 30 ⓦ www.brasserielipp.se
ⓛ 11.30–01.00 Mon–Wed, 11.30–03.00 Thur & Fri, 12.00–03.00
Sat, 12.00–24.00 Sun

Kock & Vin £££ ❾ A gourmet restaurant that's received rave reviews and a star in the Guide Michelin. Kock & Vin is quite pricey, but the Sinnenas Meny (Menu of the Senses) is nevertheless a good deal, as it contains almost half of the dishes on the regular menu. Be prepared for innovative Swedish cuisine, such as lukewarm baked Kamchatka crab with salsify and milk spiced with dill. ⓐ Viktoriagatan 12 ⓣ 031 701 79 79 ⓦ www.kockvin.com ⓛ 18.00–late

BARS & CLUBS

Dancin' Dingo Possibly the pick of Gothenburg's expat haunts, this lively Australian watering hole has live music or a DJ almost every night, a pool room, friendly bar staff and a great atmosphere. ⓐ Kristinelundsgatan 16 ⓣ 031 81 18 12 ⓦ www.dancindingo.com ⓛ 20.00–02.00 Tues–Thur, 17.00–03.00 Fri & Sat, 17.00–02.00 Sun, closed Mon ❶ Minimum age limit: 22 years

Flying Scotsman For more than a decade 'walk in, fly out' has been the motto at this faux Scottish tavern (and no, it doesn't mean on the end of a fist the minute you walk through the door). The staff are friendly, and the tartan is not overdone. There is a large selection of whiskies, but the little Swedish touches here and there remind drinkers that they're a long way from the Highlands. ⓐ Storgatan 47 ⓣ 031 13 76 46 ⓦ www.flying scotsman.se ⓛ 16.00–late Mon–Wed, 16.00–01.00 Thur, 16.00–03.00 Fri, 13.00–03.00 Sat, closed Sun

Glow If it's some hard party action you're looking for, then head straight for the nightclub next to the Brasserie Lipp where you will find countless dancing queens to take a chance on. ⓐ Kungsportsavenyn 8 ⓣ 031 10 58 20 ⓦ www.glow nightclub.se ⓛ 23.00–05.00 Fri & Sat ⓘ Minimum age: 28 years

Joe Farelli's This combination of mamma's kitchen and sleek bar will not be to everyone's taste; the backstreet-in-Naples dining area and stylish NY bar area sit somewhat incongruously side-by-side. But they do serve believable Italian food and the bar is well stocked. ⓐ Kungsportsavenyn 12 ⓣ 031 10 58 26 ⓦ www. joefarelli.com ⓛ 11.30–01.00 Mon–Wed, 11.30–02.00 Thur & Fri, 12.00–03.00 Sat, 12.00–01.00 Sun

Nivå Five pulsating floors of soul, funk and R&B greet partygoers at Nivå, one of the best clubs in the city. By day you can even retreat to the restaurant for a buffet lunch, but by night the young and beautiful strut their stuff till sunrise (not actually that difficult in summer). ⓐ Kungsportsavenyn 9 ⓣ 031 701 80 90 ⓦ www.restaurangniva.com ⓛ 22.00–03.00 Wed, 22.00–04.30 Fri & Sat ⓘ Minimum age: 25 years

Push Opened in 2008, Push quickly became the most fashionable place in town for big spenders in their mid-20s. Check out the spectacular LED lights and details such as the gorgeous all-white, Baroque-style bar. The terrace is the place to be seen during summer. ⓐ Kungsportsavenyn 11 ⓣ 031 701 80 90 ⓦ www. push.se ⓛ 22.00–04.00 Fri & Sat ⓘ Minimum age: 28 years

---

▶ *A castle with a view: Carlstens Fortress at Marstrand*

OUT OF TOWN
trips

Kungälv & Marstrand

KUNGÄLV

Kungälv, just outside Gothenburg's northern city limits, provides an easy and rewarding day trip away from the sparkling shops and general hustle and bustle of the city. The town is divided into a modern part with shops, offices and light industry, and a wonderful old village, the original medieval settlement. The picturesque village, set against steep wooded hills and rocky outcrops, can also be used as a stop-off on your way to Marstrand, 25 km (15½ miles) to the west. The main attraction is impenetrable Bohus Fortress, a hefty mountain of stone built in the 14th century on a strategic hill overlooking the place where the Göta River splits in two, but the old village itself with its pastel-coloured timber houses, some buckled and leaning over or away from the cobbled streets, is a fairy-tale sort of place and well worth an hour's exploration.

The town started life in the 10th century as the Norwegian border outpost of Kungahälla. Huddled around Bohus Fortress (which was 700 years old in 2008), the strategic frontier town withstood many sieges but gradually lost its importance during the course of the 17th century when Gothenburg was established. It became something of an overlooked backwater until the 19th century when industry arrived. Today the town draws thousands of tourists thanks to the fortress and its pretty timber architecture. In 2008, Kungälv unveiled its brand new tourist office – **Våghals Turistcenter** (ⓐ Färjevägen 2, Kungälv ⓕ 0303 189 00 ⓦ www.vaghals.se).

◯ *Typical pastel-coloured houses in Kungälv*

Norway
Sweden
Gothenburg

Marstrand

Kungälv
45
Surte

Klåverön
Nature Reserve

Gothenburg City

Lerur

Torslanda

GOTHENBURG

Mölnlycke

Gothenbu
Landvett

Lindome

Vrångö
Nature Reserve

Kungsbacka

Rydet

Åsa

○ ......City
○ ......Large Town
○ ......Small Town
══ ......Motorway
── ......Main Road
── ......Minor Road
✈ ......Airport
── ......Railway
──── ......Regional
Border

Læsø

Kattegat

Ringhals

Gothenburg
region
0 ─────── 10 km
0 ──── 5 miles

Varberg

GETTING THERE

The best way to reach Kungälv is to take the so-called Green Express (Grön Express) bus from the tram stop in front of the main tourist office in Gothenburg. Buses run every 20 minutes or so, tickets are bought from the driver, and the journey takes no more than 25 minutes. Don't forget to put your seat belt on when the coach glides on to the motorway. ❶ Get off as soon as you spot the fortress on the right; if you stay on board longer, you'll end up at Kungälv bus station and have to walk back through the modern centre to the old village.

SIGHTS & ATTRACTIONS
Bohus Fortress

Big, bold Bohus Fortress began life as a wooden hilltop structure, built in 1308 by Norwegian king Haakon V Magnusson to protect the border from marauding Swedes. Later the fortress was beefed up considerably using huge boulders, and at its peak boasted four great towers. The builders did such a good job that Bohus was never taken despite the 14 sieges and battles that followed over the centuries. It also hosted many grand royal events such as marriages and the signing of treaties. All this came to an end in the 17th century when the focus shifted to heavily fortified Gothenburg to the south, and Bohus fell into ruins. It wasn't until the late 19th century that the Swedish government saw fit to declare the ruins a national monument.

The remains of this monster of a medieval stronghold brood silently on the edge of the village as a reminder of the erstwhile strategic importance of Kungälv. The hilltop setting is dominated by a hefty round tower, and the fortress walls are like giant wedges of stone, reminiscent of the Egyptian pyramids. The views across the river and into the forested hills, which form the backdrop to the prim and proper village, are fantastic. Most visitors pay the entrance fee and scramble around the grassy ramparts, armed with a simple brochure available at the ticket booth. Those who want to take the full-blown guided tour must call ahead to book an English-speaking guide. ⓐ Kungälv ⓣ 0303 23 92 03 ⓦ www.bohusfastning.com ⓛ 11.00–17.00 Sat & Sun (Apr); 10.00–19.00 (May–Aug); 11.00–15.00 (Sept); 11.00–15.00 Sat & Sun (Oct) ⓘ Last entry half an hour before closing time. Admission charge

The village

The delicate timber architecture of the village below stands in stark contrast to the weighty presence of the stone fortress above. Kungälv's historic core basically consists of Gamla Torget, the main square, and Västra Gatan, which leads to the modern town. There are two buildings of note on the square: the first is the timber church dating from 1679, which looks simple from the outside but inside conceals beautifully painted ceilings. It is generally regarded as Sweden's most attractive Baroque wooden church. The other is the old town hall dating from 1762, which served its original purpose until the 1930s. The picturesque cobbles of the Västra Gatan snake west from the Gamla Torget to the modern town centre. Its entire length is lined with wonderful examples of traditional Swedish timber architecture of the type everyone has seen in tourist brochures and on the covers of tourist guides. At the Fars Hatt Hotel you can pick up a map explaining the history of almost every house along the route (though this was only available

in Swedish at the time of writing). Every house is painted a different pastel shade, and each has its own prim, picture-book character. Västra Gatan finally gives way to the 21st century when it swaps traditional houses for a modern shopping precinct.

RETAIL THERAPY

Kungälv high street in the modern part of town has several decent retail outlets, but nothing you won't find back in the city. If you are looking for souvenirs and nothing has caught your eye back in Gothenburg, try some of Kungälv's arts and handicrafts studios where you can pick up original works with local themes.

Ateljé Rådhuset Paintings. ⓐ Gamla Torget 1 ⓣ 073 985 24 25 ⓛ There are no regular opening hours – phone ahead to arrange a visit

Axelson Interiör Glassware, handicrafts. ⓐ Västra Gatan 71 ⓣ 0303 163 53 ⓦ www.axelsonsint.se ⓛ 10.00–18.00 Mon–Fri, 10.00–15.00 Sat, closed Sun

Galleri 37 Paintings. ⓐ Västra Gatan 37 ⓣ 073 570 44 49 ⓦ www.galleri37.se ⓛ There are no regular opening hours – phone ahead to arrange a visit

TAKING A BREAK

Many visitors on a quick stopover in Kungälv may be tempted to just grab a snack at the small kiosk in the fortress car park, surrounded by picnic tables. Otherwise, pack a picnic in Gothenburg and head down to the river, or find a scenic spot in the hills beyond the village. The Fars Hatt Hotel (see opposite) has a bar and restaurant.

ACCOMMODATION

Hostels

Kungälv Youth Hostel & Campsite £ In a great location directly across the road from the fortress car park, this attractive timber building houses a basic youth hostel. Behind it is a small campsite, though it might be hard to sleep due to the proximity of the busy road. ⓐ Färjevägen 2 ⓣ 0303 189 00 ⓦ www.kungalvsvandrar hem.se ⓒ Reception open daily 09.00–12.00, 15.00–18.30 (May & June); 08.00–21.00 (July & Aug); 09.00–12.00, 12.00–18.30 (Sept); telephone between 09.00–12.00 Mon–Fri (Oct–Apr)

Hotels

Fars Hatt Hotel ££ The Fars Hatt is the most convenient hotel for Bohus Fortress as it stands slap bang in the middle of the village square. Apart from the comfortable rooms and pleasant restaurant and bar, this is also a good place to pick up some tourist information on Kungälv and Marstrand. Reception staff will also help you with any queries you may have, even if you're not staying the night. ⓐ Torget 2 ⓣ 0303 109 70 ⓦ www.farshatt.se

MARSTRAND

Some 25 km (15½ miles) west of Kungälv along route 168 lies the tiny village of Marstrand, which hugs the shores of an island dominated by the weighty presence of yet another medieval fortress. The village, which occupies only a small fraction of the island's total area, is similar to Kungälv with its cobbled lanes and pastel-coloured timber houses. Marstrand gets its name from the

church on the island, which was once called Maria Strand (Maria's Beach) after a girl who was shipwrecked here in the 12th century.

Naturally the chief draw is **Carlstens Fortress** (@ 440 30 Marstrand ① 0303 602 65 @ www.carlsten.se ● 11.00–16.00 (1–24 June & 1–31 Aug); 11.00–18.00 (26 June–31 July), closed 25 June ① Admission charge). Like Bohus, it is an enormous slab of impenetrable stone. Under the weight of all those boulders it's a wonder the island doesn't sink into the sea. Unlike Bohus there is actually something to see inside, and guided tours run when a sufficiently large crowd of tourists gathers. The fortress only appeared on the island after the Bohuslän Coast was ceded to Sweden in the Peace of Roskilde in 1658. Marstrand had always been an important place for merchant ships, as the harbour is almost never ice-bound. It took more than 200 years to build the fortress, by which time Gothenburg had secured top spot in the area. Construction work was mainly carried out by prisoners, who had to wear a 2-kg (4½-lb) ball and chain to stop them escaping. The most famous of these was Lasse-Maja, a kind of Swedish Robin Hood, who evaded arrest by dressing up as a woman. Finally caught in 1813, he had an easy time of it at Carlstens Fortress, as he cooked for the grateful prison guards, a skill he had learnt during his time in a skirt. The prison cells, measuring a back-twisting 2 by 3 m (6½ by 10 ft) and equipped with all kinds of shackles and chains, are the creepiest, most gruesome part of the tour. The views from the 100-m (328-ft)-high tower are another highlight.

The **tourist office** (@ Hamngatan 33, Marstrand ① 0303 600 87) has an excellent website @ www.marstrand.se

⬥ *Enjoying the rock pools at Marstrand*

⬥ *The imposing fortress at Marstrand*

GETTING THERE

Renting a car to see both Marstrand and Kungälv may be your best option. However, it is not the only option: bus 312 from the Nils Ericson Coach Station runs throughout the day and takes 35 minutes to complete its journey north. Alternatively, you can take the Green Express to Kungälv bus station, then change on to bus 302. This route takes considerably longer. Marstrand is linked to the 'mainland' by ferry (which runs four times an hour daily between April and September, the trip taking a few minutes), and no cars are allowed on to the island (bear that in mind if you do rent a vehicle).

AFTER DARK

Gran Tenan Just by Paradisparken (Paradise Park), with a magnificent view of the sea, you may enjoy Tenan's famous oven-baked crayfish in an environment dating back to 1892. The building was then a summer house for King Oscar II. Everyone can enjoy this spectacular hotel-restaurant today. Booking is advisable, however. ⓐ Grand Hotel Marstrand, Rådhusgatan 2 ⓣ 030 36 03 22 ⓛ 11.00–23.00 (restaurant)

Varberg

The pretty town of Varberg is an ideal relaxing away-day destination with a peppering of historic sites, lots of secluded sandy beaches and a handful of pleasant bars and cafés. Varberg grew in the 19th century as a spa and is still one of the west coast's most popular seaside resorts. The town centre is a quaint grid of pastel-coloured timber buildings, typical for Sweden, but the main attractions are grouped together on the seafront, dominated by a huge hilltop fortress.

GETTING THERE

Getting to Varberg could not be easier. A mere 40 minutes by express train south of Gothenburg, the town straddles the Gothenburg–Malmö–Copenhagen mainline and all express trains stop here. Between one and three services an hour make the journey between Varberg and Gothenburg Central Station. Buying a ticket in advance and avoiding the X 2000 super-fast services will save you money.

SIGHTS & ATTRACTIONS

Beaches

Away from the town's historical sights, one of the principal reasons for travelling to Varberg is to catch some precious Scandinavian sun on the fabulous beaches. Near the fortress, the coastline is rocky and uninviting, but 1 km (½ mile) further south around Apelviken Bay it opens out into beautiful golden

◒ *Varberg's Kallbadhuset offers cold baths, hot saunas and a café*

sand, the ideal place for a picnic when the Norse weather gods permit. There are also two single-sex nudist beaches to the south of the area.

Kallbadhuset (Cold Bathhouse Spa)

Down by the sea below the fortress, the Cold Bathhouse Spa juts out into the briny like a miniature version of Brighton Pavilion on stilts. The timber pier-cum-sauna is one of Sweden's most delightful buildings and was created in 1902 with obvious oriental influences. Even if you don't fancy naked bathing inside (men and women separately of course), chill out for half an hour over coffee and cakes in the quaint little café just inside the building.
ⓐ Ymergatan 30 ⓦ www.kallbadhuset.se (in Swedish only)
🕒 09.00–18.00 Thur–Tues, 09.00–20.00 Wed (mid-June–mid-Aug)

Town centre

Your first port of call should most definitely be Varberg's efficient tourist office, a few hundred metres from the railway station. Pick up a free map of the town and set off towards the church to explore. The main square, called Stortorget, is the focal point for life in Varberg; in summer it is awash with cafés and market stalls and, before Christmas, yuletide markets clutter its expanse. The streets that radiate away from it are notable for their two-storey timber structures, most of which house shops and offices.

Varberg tourist office ⓐ Västra Vallgatan 39 ⓣ 0340 868 00
ⓦ www.visitvarberg.se 🕒 10.00–17.00 Mon–Fri (Jan–Apr & Sept–Dec); 10.00–17.00 Mon–Fri, 10.00–15.00 Sat (May & June); 09.30–19.00 Mon–Sat, 13.00–18.00 Sun (July & Aug)

CULTURE

Varberg Fortress & Museum

Sitting defiantly atop a rocky promontory overlooking the sea, Varberg Fortress is the town's most significant attraction. Built in the 13th century, it changed hands several times between the Danes and Swedes until 1645 when the area finally came under Swedish control for good.

The beefy ramparts now protect a museum where the most interesting and important exhibit is the Bocksten Man. Dug up by a farmer in 1936, Bocksten Man, named after the farm 25 km (15½ miles) east of Varberg, had been murdered and thrown into a bog 600 years earlier and was still dressed in one of the most complete medieval costumes ever found in Europe. To stop his spirit coming back to haunt them, the murderers pierced the body with three stakes. Today he is an eerie sight, though many still buy a key ring or other souvenir adorned with an image of the corpse in the gift shop afterwards.

Other exhibitions include a button from the uniform of King Karl XII, fired from a gun to assassinate him, a section on the local farming and fishing industries and an art gallery housing paintings in the so-called Varberg School, with pieces by local 19th-century artists Richard Bergh, Karl Nordström and Nils Kreuger. The works depict Varberg and other rural scenes from Halland province.

Museum ⓐ Fästningen 432 ⓣ 0340 828 30 ⓦ www.lansmuseet. varberg.se ⓛ 10.00–16.00 Mon–Fri, 12.00–16.00 Sat & Sun ⓘ Admission charge

◐ *Inside the walls of Varberg Fortress, the museum houses the Bocksten Man*

Varberg Fortress Prison

A few steps down the hill from the fortress stands a former prison, now a youth hostel. Built in the mid-19th century, it housed prisoners serving life sentences for murder until the 1930s. Today it's one of the best locations in town to spend the night (see page 120).

RETAIL THERAPY

Almost every building in the town centre seems to be a shop, but you won't find anything here that you can't buy in Gothenburg. One place you might find some interesting and unusual items is Varberg market, held every Wednesday and Saturday on the Stortorget.

TAKING A BREAK

Blå Dörren Kafé £ Popular and recommended by the locals, the 'Blue Door' is housed in a low timber building on the corner of Norrgatan and the main drag from the station. The rule in Sweden is that if a place fills up at lunchtime, it serves good, affordable food; this place is normally chock-a-block. ⓐ Norrgatan 1 ⓣ 0340 67 34 40 ⓛ 09.00–19.00 Mon–Fri, 10.00–17.30 Sat & Sun

Majas vid havet £–££ Another local favourite, this time around 2 km (1¼ miles) south of the main square in Apelviken Bay. Open only in the summer months, there is live music most nights, and people come from miles around to sample the cuisine. ⓐ Apelvikens Strand ⓣ 0340 141 51 ⓔ info@majas.nu ⓛ Summer only

AFTER DARK

Harry's Pub £–££ Varberg's best bar and pub-style restaurant is part of a chain with branches across Sweden. It may have a confused blend of décor (cherubs and old posters) but the food is relatively cheap and there are Czech Staropramen and Guinness® on tap. An excellent place for lunch or an *öl* (beer) session of an evening. ⓐ Kungsgatan 18 ⓣ 0340 872 85 ⓦ http://varberg.harryspubar.se ⓛ 16.00–23.00 Mon & Tues, 16.00–01.00 Wed, 16.00–24.00 Thur, 16.00–02.00 Fri, 12.00–02.00 Sat, closed Sun

Beer n' Bar ££ Of the two nightspots that face each other where Borgmästaregatan and Kungsgatan intersect, Beer n' Bar is the more expensive and upmarket and attracts a more mature crowd. There's a laid-back atmosphere and the seafood is second to none in Varberg. ⓐ Kungsgatan 13 ⓣ 0340 898 99 ⓦ www.justme.se/bb ⓛ 11.00–14.30 Mon, 11.00–14.30, 18.00–23.00 Tues–Thur, 11.00–02.00 Fri & Sat, 12.00–24.00 Sun

ACCOMMODATION

HOSTELS

Fästningens Vandrarhem £ For some perverted reason folk just love staying in former prisons. It must be the powerless fantasy feeling of being locked up in a cell, combined with the knowledge that you are free to walk out of the door whenever you like. If you're into this sort of thing, Varberg's youth hostel is the place to stay. Many of the rooms in the main building have changed

● Fishing boats line the coast at Varberg

little since they housed lifers. ⓐ Varbergs Fästning ⓣ 0340 868 28
ⓦ www.fastningensvandrarhem.se

HOTELS

Hotell Gästis ££ The Gästis is a cosy place to stay, with a variety
of rooms in all shapes, sizes and décors. The 18th-century cellar is
now a spa, including a weird but wonderful copy of Lenin's bath.
Breakfast is included. ⓐ Borgmästaregatan 1 ⓣ 0340 180 50
ⓦ www.hotellgastis.nu

Hotell Varberg ££ More affordable than the other three
establishments listed here, the Varberg is aimed at a younger
market. Rooms are basic but functional and spotless. Breakfast is
included. ⓐ Norrgatan 16 ⓣ 0340 161 25 ⓦ www.hotellvarberg.nu

BED & BREAKFAST

Okéns Bed & Breakfast ££ This friendly, family-run B&B is good
value for money, and perfect if you like kitschy, romantically
furnished rooms with canopy beds and copious lace
decorations. ⓐ Västra Vallgatan 25 ⓣ 0340 808 15
ⓦ www.okens.se

● *The Älvsborg bridge connects Gothenburg city with Hisingen island*

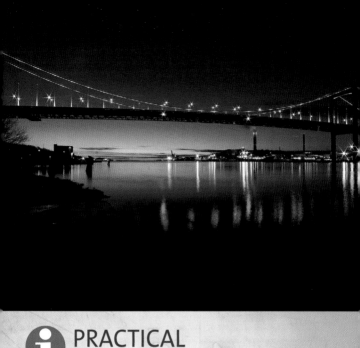

PRACTICAL
information

Directory

GETTING THERE

By air

Two airlines link the UK with Gothenburg-Landvetter Airport: the budget operator City Airline and the pan-Scandinavian carrier, SAS. The former operates flights from Birmingham and Manchester, while SAS shuttles passengers to and from Heathrow. Ryanair runs services from Dublin, Stansted and Glasgow. These arrive and depart from tiny Gothenburg City Airport.

Long-haul passengers would normally take their own country's airline or an SAS flight to Stockholm and then continue to Gothenburg on an SAS domestic service or by train or coach. Flights to Copenhagen are also a good option since there are excellent air and rail connections between the two cities.

City Airline ⓦ www.cityairline.com

Gothenburg City Airport ⓦ www.goteborgairport.se

Gothenburg-Landvetter Airport ⓦ www.lfv.se

Ryanair ⓦ www.ryanair.com

SAS ⓦ www.scandinavian.net

Many people are aware that air travel emits CO_2, which contributes to climate change. You may be interested in the possibility of lessening the environmental impact of your flight through the charity **Climate Care** (ⓦ www.jpmorganclimatecare.com), which offsets your CO_2 by funding environmental projects around the world.

By rail

SJ (Statens Järnvägar) runs the trains all over Sweden. The service is clean, comfortable, efficient and expensive. Gothenburg has direct rail connections to Oslo, Copenhagen, Malmö and Stockholm.

🔺 *Trams trundle their way through the city streets*

By road

There are coach services to many cities in Sweden as well as Eurolines connections to places in western and eastern Europe. When arriving and departing by bus, the Nils Ericson Coach Station is situated directly behind the Central Railway Station, almost in the same building.

By water

Since the demise of the Newcastle–Gothenburg ferry, a Gothenburg institution since the 19th century, slightly fewer people will now arrive by boat. That said, **Stena Line** ferries (ⓦ www.stenaline.se) still arrive from various places across Scandinavia and northern Germany.

ENTRY FORMALITIES

Sweden is a fully paid-up, though not overenthusiastic, member of the EU and is party to the Schengen Agreement; all good news for travellers who like it easy at borders. Basically, citizens from other EU countries can stay indefinitely, and those from the US, Canada, Australia and New Zealand can remain in the country for a certain length of time. Holders of South African passports need a visa. If you need a Schengen visa to visit Sweden, contact your nearest Swedish embassy to find out what you'll need in order to apply.

MONEY

Sweden's currency is the krona (plural kronor), abbreviated to 'kr' or SEK. There are a hundred öre in one krona.

Plastic is accepted everywhere you would expect it to be at home, and there is never a fuss in Sweden when someone slides a card from his or her wallet or purse. You may be surprised to see the bus driver of the airport express bus swiping cards. The chip and PIN method of payment is becoming increasingly widespread, though the terminals sometimes require you to swipe the card instead of inserting it into the slot.

Cash machines (ATMs or *bankomater*) are almost as common as in Britain and the US and take all major credit and debit cards. They can be found in the main shopping centres, the airport and in main streets such as the Kungsportsavenyn. This is by far the best way to access your account in Sweden, as long as you know your PIN.

If you have bought an item in Sweden worth more than SEK 200, and you are flying out of the EU, you are eligible to a VAT refund. Present the goods (unused and with the price tags attached), your passport and ticket/boarding pass, Global Refund receipt and the shop receipt to customs at the airport.
Global Blue ⓦ www.global-blue.com

TIPPING

Greasing palms is not mandatory, but if you are satisfied with the food, drink and service, ten per cent of the bill is the norm. Many round up the bill to the nearest ten krona or leave any one- or five-krona pieces they receive in their change on the table or bar, but this is considered mean. Taxi drivers appreciate passengers rounding up the fare to a neat sum, so they don't have to waste time fishing around for loose change. A service charge is usually included in the bill at sit-down restaurants.

Forex (ⓦ www.forex.se) is the largest foreign-exchange company in Scandinavia and has seven conveniently located branches in Gothenburg (including at the airport, Kungsportsavenyn 22, the Central Station, the Nordstan shopping centre and the Kungsportsplatsen, almost opposite the tourist information office). They are the easiest and most user-friendly places to convert your pounds, dollars, euros and 80 other currencies into kronor.

HEALTH, SAFETY & CRIME

Health and safety in Sweden are among the highest in the world, with the vast majority of safety and food-hygiene regulations surpassing levels acceptable in the EU. Tap water is safe to drink, and tastes quite good.

Road safety can be an issue when you are in Gothenburg. Make sure you are standing on your designated part of the street to avoid being mown down by a bike, car or tram, which will not expect you to be on its part of the street. Driving in Sweden can be a great experience, though watch out for bad weather and icy or snowy conditions.

Swedish healthcare is of the highest standard and, should you be unfortunate enough to find yourself in a Swedish hospital, you will be well looked after. Those from the EU holding EHICs (European Health Insurance Cards) receive emergency treatment free of charge. Non-EU nationals should make sure they take out the necessary health insurance.

Violent crime is rare and most offences concern petty theft; the basic advice to visitors is to use common sense and take the same precautions as you would to stay safe back home.

OPENING HOURS

Attractions 🕐 09.00 or 10.00–17.00 or 18.00

Banks 🕐 09.30–15.00 Mon–Fri; large city branches 09.30–18.00 Mon–Fri

Office hours 🕐 09.00–17.00 Mon–Fri

Shops 🕐 09.00–18.00 Mon–Fri, 09.00–16.00 Sat; larger city stores 12.00–16.00 Sun

TOILETS

Spending a penny in Sweden can end up costing a bomb on longer stays. Free public conveniences are few and far between (though they do exist), and most have a coin-devouring box, which unlocks the door. And don't think you'll be popping into McDonald's™ or Burger King® for a free visit, as they cleverly charge the same (5 kronor). As with most things in Sweden, the high charge results in a very high standard, and a bad public toilet is almost unheard of (though some of the free ones are on the nasty side). The only places you are certain of finding free loos are on trains, at the airport and in most restaurants. Toilets are marked with the familiar figures of a man and woman, and confusing the two is unlikely (unless you've had too much *öl*).

CHILDREN

Gothenburg has a lot for children to enjoy and Sweden in general is a very child-friendly country. Swedes like children, and if an attraction isn't aimed directly at the kiddies, there will usually be an exhibit or space set aside especially to keep them entertained. Children's portions, menus and high chairs come as standard in almost every café and restaurant. Health and safety where children are concerned could not be a higher priority in Sweden, and you can rest assured that equipment such as playground rides is of the highest standard in the world. Under-sevens ride free on all public transport, and all trams have large pram bays. Getting on and off the trams with a pram or pushchair is easy and can usually be achieved without assistance.

The obvious top attraction for children is **Liseberg Amusement Park** (see page 91), but Gothenburg possesses several other less obvious attractions when you have the wee ones in tow. The **Children's Zoo** (see page 79) in the Slottsskogen gives youngsters the chance to interact with farm animals in an enclosure where both can wander freely. The zoo also keeps penguins and flamingos. Kids will also love the excitement of the **Paddan boat cruises** (see page 58), the open spaces of Gothenburg's numerous parks and the exhibits at the **Universeum (Science Museum)** (see page 93).

COMMUNICATIONS
Internet
Gothenburg has a good number of Internet cafés. Sweden has actually got the highest percentage of Internet users in the world, so almost all Swedes surf via their own private laptops, mobile phones, or both. If you have an iPhone or BlackBerry, you can find the nearest Internet café by typing in
ⓦ www.wifikartan.se and identifying your location. Alternatively, just head for Gothenburg's public library at the top end of the Kungsportsavenyn, where even non-residents can use any of the numerous computers for one hour free of charge. Take your passport and register at the

front desk (staff speak English). The process takes around ten minutes.

Wi-Fi hotspots are well established in Gothenburg and can be found as standard in almost all upmarket hotels, some three-star establishments and at the airport.

The Swedish website prefix is .se, though .nu and .com are also common.

Phone

Sweden's principal landline telephone operator is Telia. Most people now use mobiles, and as Sweden uses the GSM system, handsets from the UK and other European countries will work the same as they do at home. Phones from the US and Canada may not, and Australian and New Zealand handsets need a change of band frequency.

TELEPHONING SWEDEN

The country code for Sweden is 0046. To ring a number in Gothenburg from abroad, dial 0046 31 then the five-/six-/seven-digit number.

To call Gothenburg from within Sweden, dial 031 then the five-/six-/seven-digit number.

TELEPHONING ABROAD

To make an international call from Sweden, dial 00 then the code for the country you wish to call, followed by the subscriber number.

Post

The Swedish high-street post office was resigned to the scrap heap of history in the early part of this decade, with postal-service centres being reopened at petrol stations and food shops, the argument being that they could open longer hours. The move has proved unpopular, though this may just be Sweden leading the way in what might become inevitable in many other European countries. As a visitor you may never actually need a post office anyway, as stamps can also be bought at most newsagents, hotels and stationery shops. The Swedish postal system is generally very efficient.

Swedish Post Office Ⓦ www.posten.se

ELECTRICITY

Sweden works on 220 V AC, 50 Hz. To use electrical appliances from home you will need a continental two-pin adaptor. Laptops from the US using only 110 V will need a transformer.

TRAVELLERS WITH DISABILITIES

Gothenburg is a very wheelchair-friendly city and getting around, eating and sleeping should only pose as many problems here as they do in the UK and the US. Most hotels have good disabled facilities, with top-end establishments providing access to all areas, including swimming pools and spa facilities. Restaurants and cafés, especially those with steps down from the pavement, aren't always ideal for wheelchair-users, though the vast majority now have ramps. Public transport poses few problems, especially when it comes to the tourist's most common mode of transport – the tram. Trams are low enough to get a wheelchair on to, perhaps with a little assistance from your travelling companions, and they have spacious wheelchair bays once you're on board.

The national disabled association in Sweden is called the Handikappades Riksförbund and is based in Stockholm. You're advised to contact them for any further information on disabled access in Sweden. The Gothenburg tourist office can also answer queries on the facilities offered by individual premises.

Handikappades Riksförbund ⓐ Slottskogsgatan 12, Stockholm ⓣ 031 367 98 30 ⓦ www.dhr.segoteborg

DRIVING

When the weather is fine, driving in Gothenburg and indeed Sweden in general is sheer joy. Road surfaces as smooth as unassembled IKEA flat-packs, traffic-free motorways, clear road markings and generally competent and polite fellow road-users make it a motorist's heaven. However, the problems sometimes start for foreign drivers when the heavens open up, especially in winter. Experience of driving on snow and ice is recommended, and most Swedish vehicles are fitted with studded tyres in winter, which scratch the roads clean when there's no snow for them to dig their fangs into. If you are bringing your car from the UK, where for some odd reason this sort of tyre is banned, you could have problems staying on the road in the worst of the winter weather.

Sadly for UK drivers, Sweden switched to driving on the right in 1967, but other than that, there are few specific issues (apart from the weather) for foreign motorists. In city streets, look out for trams and cycles, which sometimes have right of way when you wouldn't expect it. Watch out for boarding and alighting passengers at tram stops and for cyclists where cycle paths cross roads. ⓘ Dipped headlights should be used at all times

TOURIST INFORMATION

Tourist information centres can be found in the following locations:

Main Office ⓐ Kungsportsplatsen 2 ⓣ 031 61 25 00
ⓦ www.goteborg.com

Branch Office ⓐ Nordstan shopping centre ⓣ 031 700 86 60

The main office at the Kungsportsplatsen should be your first point of reference. The English-speaking staff are very welcoming and will assist you with any query you may have about their city. City maps and a basic guide are available, though that's pretty much where the freebies end. The office also sells souvenirs, books and more detailed maps.

The tourist offices are also the best places to get your essential **Gothenburg Pass**. This is a card costing around SEK 245 a day, which gives the holder heaps of discounts at shops and restaurants, free admission to many of the city's attractions, free transport around Gothenburg (including ferries) and numerous two-for-the-price-of-one offers. It's amazing value for money and will save you a fortune if you intend to see a lot during your stay. McDonald's™ will even give you a free cheeseburger – now there's an offer you can't refuse!

The Gothenburg Package combines a night's hotel accommodation with a Gothenburg Pass. This starts at SEK 620, but the price depends on the hotel you choose to stay in. Often the hotel room costs less with the Gothenburg Pass than without it. Ask at the tourist office.

BACKGROUND READING

The tourist office publishes an annual *Official Tourist Guide to Gothenburg*, which is handed out free of charge. Its website
ⓦ www.goteborg.com also has tons of information on all aspects of the city. Otherwise, not a great deal has ever been written about Gothenburg, despite its British connections.

Emergencies

EMERGENCY NUMBERS

To call an ambulance, the police or the fire brigade, simply call
☎ 112. This is the pan-European emergency number, which many
other EU countries have yet to adopt.

POLICE

Main Police Station **☎** 114 14 (24 hours)

MEDICAL SERVICES

Emergency healthcare is available from:
Capio Axess Akuten **ⓐ** Södra Allégatan 6 **☎** 031 725 00 50
ⓦ www.capioaxessakuten.se
CityAkuten **ⓐ** Nordstadstorget 6 **☎** 031 10 10 10
ⓦ www.cityakuten.se

Emergency dental care is available from:
Tandvården Göteborg **ⓐ** Akuttandvården, Odinsgatan 10
☎ 031 80 78 00

IAMAT is a not-for-profit organisation that disseminates information
on travel-related health issues. Access the website for a list of
English-speaking doctors in Gothenburg. **ⓦ** www.iamat.org

ROADSIDE ASSISTANCE

Assistancekåren is a network of 150 salvage firms and is the only
Swedish company to offer motor assistance nationwide.
☎ 020 912 912 (24 hours) **ⓦ** www.assistancekaren.se

EMERGENCY PHRASES

Fire!	**Help!**	**Stop!**
Det brinner!	Hjälp!	Stopp!
Det brinner!	*Yelp!*	*Stop!*

Get a doctor!	**Call the police!**	**Call an ambulance!**
Hämta en läkare!	Ring polisen!	Ring en ambulans!
Hemta en lairkare!	*Ring pooleesen!*	*Ring en ambulans!*

EMBASSIES & CONSULATES

The British Consulate General closed in December 2006, probably thanks to the termination of the ferry, which used to operate between Newcastle and Gothenburg. The embassy in Stockholm now handles all enquiries from British citizens. Americans, Australians and New Zealanders should also contact their embassies in the capital.

Australia ⓐ Sergels Torg 12, 11th Floor, Stockholm ⓣ 08 613 29 00

New Zealand ⓐ Regus Centre, Stureplan 4C, Stockholm ⓣ 08 463 10 00

UK ⓐ Skarpögatan 6–8, Stockholm ⓣ 08 671 30 00 ⓦ www.britishembassy.se

US ⓐ Dag Hammarskjölds Väg 31, Stockholm ⓣ 08 783 53 00 ⓦ http://stockholm.usembassy.gov

ACKNOWLEDGEMENTS

The publishers would like to thank the following individuals and organisations for supplying their copyright photographs for this book:

Alamy, pages 57 & 118; Big Stock Photo (Antony McAulay, page 14; Erik Englesson, page 19); Stuart Chalmers, page 34; Marc Di Duca, pages 23, 45, 49, 63, 81, 87, 97, 103, 115, 121 & 125; Dreamstime (Sandra Kemppainen, page 55; Aleksandr Bondarchiuk, page 101; Christian Westerberg Morales, page 123); Gothenburg Tourist Board (Göran Assner, pages 13, 17, 30, 65 & 111; Kjell Holmner, pages 7, 21, 40–41, 72 & 75; Bo Kågerud, page 38; Stig Kälvelid, page 32; Lars Kérla, pages 42 & 112; Roberto Rinaldi, page 75); Monika Kostera, page 47; Pictures Colour Library pages 69 & 95; Lauri Väin, page 91; Wikimedia Commons (Harn Blomberg), page 8.

Project editor: Penny Isaac
Layout: Trevor Double
Proofreaders: Karolin Thomas & Cath Senker

Send your thoughts to
books@thomascook.com

- Found a great bar, club, shop or must-see sight that we don't feature?

- Like to tip us off about any information that needs a little updating?

- Want to tell us what you love about this handy little guidebook and more importantly how we can make it even handier?

Then here's your chance to tell all! Send us ideas, discoveries and recommendations today and then look out for your valuable input in the next edition of this title.

Email the above address (stating the title) or write to:
pocket guides Series Editor, Thomas Cook Publishing, PO Box 227, Coningsby Road, Peterborough PE3 8SB, UK.

WHAT'S IN YOUR GUIDEBOOK?

Independent authors Impartial up-to-date information from our travel experts who meticulously source local knowledge.

Experience Thomas Cook's 165 years in the travel industry and guidebook publishing enriches every word with expertise you can trust.

Travel know-how Thomas Cook has thousands of staff working around the globe, all living and breathing travel.

Editors Travel-publishing professionals, pulling everything together to craft a perfect blend of words, pictures, maps and design.

You, the traveller We deliver a practical, no-nonsense approach to information, geared to how you really use it.

Useful phrases

English	Swedish	Approx pronunciation
BASICS		
Yes	Ja	*Yaa*
No	Nej	*Nay*
Please	..., tack	*..., tuck*
Thank you	Tack	*Tuck*
Hello	Hej	*Hay*
Goodbye	Hej då	*Hay daw*
Excuse me	Ursäkta	*Eurshekta*
Sorry!	Förlåt mig!	*Furlawt may!*
Don't mention it	Ingen orsak	*Ingen oorshaak*
I don't understand	Jag förstår inte	*Yaag furstawr inteh*
Do you speak English?	Talar ni engelska?	*Taalar nee engelska?*
Good morning	God morgon	*Goo morron*
Good afternoon	God middag	*Goo middag*
Good evening	God afton	*Goo afton*
Goodnight	God natt	*Goo nut*
My name is ...	Mitt namn är ...	*Mit namn air ...*
NUMBERS		
One	Ett	*Et*
Two	Två	*Tvaw*
Three	Tre	*Treh*
Four	Fyra	*Fewra*
Five	Fem	*Fem*
Six	Sex	*Sex*
Seven	Sju	*Sheu*
Eight	Åtta	*Otta*
Nine	Nio	*Neeoo*
Ten	Tio	*Teeoo*
Eleven	Elva	*Elva*
Twelve	Tolv	*Tolv*
Twenty	Tjugo	*Cheugoo*
Fifty	Femtio	*Femteeoo*
One hundred	Ett hundra	*Et heundra*
SIGNS & NOTICES		
Airport	Flygplats	*Flewg-plats*
Rail station	Järnvägsstationen	*Yairnvairgs-stashoonen*
Platform	Plattform	*Platform*
Smoking/No smoking	Rökare/Icke-rökare	*Rurkareh/Ickeh-rurkareh*
Toilets	Toaletten	*Tooaletten*
Tramway	Spårvagn	*Spawr-vangn*